THE PRACTICE OF THE LOVE OF JESUS CHRIST

ST. ALPHONSUS LIGUORI

SENSUS FIDELIUM PRESS
Gastonia, North Carolina

ISBN: 978-1-962639-28-6

For more information, please visit sensusfideliumpress.com

CONTENTS

— · —

INTRODUCTION

I.

How deserving Jesus Christ is of our Love, on Account of the Love He has shown us in His Passion.

The whole sanctity and perfection of a soul consists in loving Jesus Christ, our God, our sovereign good, and our Redeemer. Whoever loves me, says Jesus Christ himself, shall be loved by my Eternal Father: My Father loves you because you have loved Me.[1] Some, says St. Francis de Sales,[2] make perfection consist in an austere life; others in prayer; others in frequenting the Sacraments; others in alms-deeds. But they deceive themselves: perfection consists in loving God with our whole heart. The Apostle wrote: Above all things, ... have charity, which is the bond of perfection.[3] It is charity which keeps united and preserves all the virtues that render a man perfect. Hence St. Augustine said: "Love God and do whatever you please;"[4] because a soul that loves God is taught by that same love never to do anything that will displease him, and to leave nothing undone that may please him.

But perhaps God does not deserve all our love? He has loved us with an everlasting love.[5] O man, says the Lord, behold I was the first to love thee. Thou wast not yet in the world, nay, the world itself was not, and I already loved thee. As long as I am God, I loved thee; as long as I have loved myself, I have also loved thee. With good reason, therefore, did St. Agnes, that young holy virgin, reply to those who wished to unite her to an earthly spouse: "I am engaged to another lover."[6] "Go," said she, "O lovers of this world, cease to sue my love; my God was the first to love me. He has loved me from all eternity: it is but just, then, for me to give him all my affections, and to love none other but him."

As Almighty God knew that man is won by kindness, he determined to lavish his gifts upon him, and so take captive the affections of his heart. For this reason, he said, I will draw them with the cords of Adam, with the bands of love.[7] I will catch men by those very snares by which they are naturally caught, that is, by the snares of love. And such exactly are all the favors of God to man. After having given him a soul created in his own image, with memory, understanding, and will, and a body with its senses, he created heaven and earth for him, yes, all that exists, all for the love of man, the firmament, the stars, the planets, the seas, the rivers, the fountains, the hills, the plains, metals, fruits, and a countless variety of animals: and all these creatures that they might minister to the uses of man, and that man might love him in gratitude for so many admirable gifts.

"Heaven and earth, and all things, tell me to love Thee,"[8] says St. Augustine. "My Lord," he said, "whatever I behold on the earth, or above the earth, all speak to me, and exhort me to love Thee; because all assure me that Thou hast made them for the love of me."

The Abbot de Rancé, founder of La Trappe, when from his hermitage he stood and surveyed the hills, the fountains, the birds, the flowers, the planets, and the skies, felt himself animated by each one of these creatures to love that God who had created all through love to him.

In like manner St. Mary Magdalene of Pazzi, when she held any beautiful flower in her hand, was enkindled by the sight of it with love to God; and she would say: "And God, then, has thought from all eternity of creating this flower for love of me!" Thus, did that flower become, as it were, a dart of love, which sweetly wounded her, and united her more and more to her God.

On the other hand, St. Teresa, at the sight of trees, fountains, rivers, lakes, or meadows, declared that all these fair things upbraided her for her ingratitude in loving so coldly a God who created them that he might be loved by her.

To the like purpose is it related of a pious hermit, that when walking through the country, it seemed to him that the plants and flowers in his path reproached him for the cold return of love he made to God; so that he went along gently striking them with his staff, and saying to them: "Oh, be silent, be silent; you call me an ungrateful wretch; you tell me

God has made you for love of me, and yet I do not love him; but now I understand you, be silent, be silent; do not reproach me more."

But God was not satisfied with giving us so many beautiful creatures. He has gone to such lengths to gain our love, as to give himself to us. The Eternal Father did not hesitate to give us even his only-begotten Son: For God so fared the world as to give His only-begotten Son.[9] When the Eternal Father saw that we were all dead, and deprived of his grace by sin, what did he do? for the immense love, nay, as the Apostle writes, for the too great love he bore us, he sent his beloved Son to make atonement for us; and so to restore to us that life which sin had robbed us of: Who through his exceeding charity with which He loved us, even when we were dead in sins, hath quickened us together in Christ.[10] And in granting us his Son (not sparing his Son, that he might spare us), he has granted us every good together with him, his grace, his love, and paradise, since assuredly all these gifts are much less than that of his Son: He that spared not even His own Son, but delivered Him tip for its all, how hath He not also with Him given us all things.[11]

And so, likewise, the Son, through his love towards us, has given himself wholly to us: Who loved me, and de livered Himself for me.[12] In order to redeem us from everlasting death, and to recover for us the divine grace and heaven which we had forfeited, he became man, and put on flesh like our own: And the Word was made flesh.[13] Be hold, then, a God reduced to nothingness: But emptied Himself, taking the form of a servant, ... and in habit found as a man.[14] Behold the sovereign of the world humbling himself so low as to assume the form of a servant, and to subject himself to all the miseries which the rest of men endure.

But what is more astonishing still is, that he could very well have saved us without dying and without suffering at all; but no: he chose a life of sorrow and contempt, and a death of bitterness and ignominy even to the expiring on a cross, the gibbet of infamy, the award of vilest criminals: He humbled Himself, becoming obedient unto death, even to the death of the cross.[15] But why, if he could have ransomed us without suffering, why should he choose to die, and to die on a cross? To show us how he loved us. He loved us and delivered Himself for us.[16] He loved us, and because he loved us, he delivered himself up to sorrows, and ignominies, and to a death more cruel than ever any man endured in this world.

Hence that great lover of Jesus Christ, St. Paul, took occasion to say: The charity of Christ presses us.[17] Wishing to show us by these words that it is not so much the sufferings themselves of Jesus Christ as his love in enduring them, that obliges us, and, as it were, constrains us to love him. Let us hear what St. Francis de Sales says on this text: "When we remember that Jesus Christ, true God, has loved us to such an excess as to suffer death, and the death of the cross, for us, our hearts are, as it were, put in a wine-press, and suffer violence, until love be extorted from them, but a violence which, the stronger it is, becomes the more delightful."[18] He then goes on to say, "Ah! why do we not therefore cast ourselves on Jesus crucified, to die on the cross with him, who has chosen to die for love of us? I will hold him (should we say), and I will never let him go; I will die with him and will be consumed in the flames of his love. One flame shall consume this divine Creator and his miserable creature. My Jesus gives himself unreservedly to me, and I give myself unreservedly to him. I will live and die on his loving breast; neither life nor death shall ever separate me from him. O eternal love, my soul longs after Thee, and makes choice of Thee forever. Come, O Holy Spirit, and inflame our hearts with love. O love, O death, to die to all other loves, to live solely to that of Jesus Christ! O Redeemer of our souls, grant that we may eternally sing, Live, Jesus! I love Jesus; live, Jesus, whom I love! yes, I love Jesus, who reigns for evermore."[19]

The love of Jesus Christ towards men created in him a longing desire for the moment of his death, when his love should be fully manifested to them; hence he was wont to say in his lifetime: I have a baptism wherewith I am to be baptized, and how am I straitened till it be accomplished![20] I have to be baptized in my own blood; and how do I feel myself straitened with the desire that the hour of my Passion may soon arrive; for then man will know the love which I bare him! Hence St. John, speaking of that night in which Jesus began his Passion, writes: Jesus knowing that His hour was come, that He should pass out of this world to the Father, having loved His own who were in the world, He loved them unto the end.[21] The Redeemer called that hour His own hour, because the time of his death was the time desired by him; as it was then that he wished to give mankind the last proof of his love, by dying for them upon a cross overwhelmed by sorrows.

But what could have ever induced a God to die as a malefactor upon a cross between two sinners, with such insult to his divine majesty? "Who did this?" asks St. Bernard; he answers, "It was love, careless of its dignity."[22] Ah, love indeed, when it tries to make itself known, does not seek what is becoming to the dignity of the lover, but what will serve best to declare itself to the object loved. St. Francis of Paula therefore had good reason to cry out at the sight of a crucifix, "O charity, O charity, O charity!" And in like manner, when we look upon Jesus on the cross, we should all exclaim, O love, O love, O love!

Ah, if faith had not assured us of it, who could ever have believed that a God, almighty, most happy, and the Lord of all, should have condescended to love man to such an extent that he seems to go out of himself for the love of him? We have seen Wisdom itself, that is the Eternal Word, become foolish through the excessive love he bore to man! So spoke St. Laurence Justinian: "We see Wisdom itself infatuated through excess of love."[23] St. Mary Magdalene of Pazzi said the same: One day, being in ecstasy, she took a wooden crucifix in her hands, and then cried out: "Yes, my Jesus, Thou art mad with love: I repeat it, and I will say it forever: My Jesus, thou art mad with love." But no, says St. Denis the Areopagite; "no, it is not madness, but the ordinary effect of divine love, which makes him who loves go out of himself, in order to give himself up entirely to the object of his love: divine love causes ecstasy."[24]

Oh, if men would only pause and consider, looking at Jesus on the cross, the love that he has borne each one of them! "With what love," says St. Francis de Sales, "would not our souls become enkindled at the sight of those flames which are in the Redeemer's breast! And oh, what happiness, to be able to be consumed by that same fire with which our God burns for us! What joy, to be united to God by the chains of love!" St. Bonaventure called the wounds of Jesus Christ, wounds which pierce the most senseless hearts, and which inflame the iciest souls.[25] How many darts of love come forth from those wounds, to wound the hardest hearts! Oh, what flames issue from the burning heart of Jesus Christ to inflame the coldest souls! And chains, how many, from that wounded side, to bind the most stubborn wills!

The Venerable John of Avila, who was so possessed with the love of Jesus Christ that he never failed in any of his sermons to speak of the love which Jesus Christ bears towards us, in a treatise on the love which this most loving Redeemer has for men, has expressed himself in sentiments so full of the fire of devotion, and of such beauty, that I desire to insert them here. He says as follows:

"Thou, O Redeemer, hast loved man in such a manner, that whoso reflects upon this love cannot do less than love Thee; for Thy love offers violence to hearts: as the Apostle says: The charity of Christ presses us.[26] The source of the love of Jesus Christ for men is his love for God. Hence, he said on Maunday Thursday, That the world may know that I love the Father, arise, let us go hence.[27] But whither? To die for men upon the cross."

"No human intellect can conceive how strongly this fire burns in the heart of Jesus Christ. As he was commanded to suffer death once, so, had he been commanded to die a thousand times, his love had been sufficient to endure it. And if what he suffered for all men had been imposed upon him for the salvation of one single soul, he would have done the same for each in particular as he did for all. And as he remained three hours upon the cross, so, had it been necessary, his love would have made him remain there even to the day of judgment. So that Jesus Christ loved much more than he suffered. O divine love, how far greater wert thou than thou outwardly seem to be; for though so many wounds and bruises tell us of great love, still they do not tell all its greatness. There was far more within than that which appeared externally. That was but as a spark which bounded forth from the vast ocean of infinite love. This is the greatest mark of love, to lay down our life for our friends. But this was not a sufficient mark for Jesus Christ wherewith to express his love."

"This is the love which causes holy souls to lose themselves, and to stand amazed, when once they have been allowed to know it. From it spring those burning sentiments of ardor, the desire of martyrdom, joy in sufferings, exultation under the storms of distress, the force to walk on burning coals as if they were roses, a thirst for sufferings, rejoicing in that which the world dreads, embracing that which it abhors. St. Ambrose says that the soul, which is espoused to Jesus Christ upon the cross, thinks nothing so glorious as to bear upon itself the marks of the crucified one."

"But how, O my lover, shall I repay this your love! It is right that blood should be compensated by blood. May I behold myself dyed in this blood and nailed to this cross! O holy cross, receive me also! O crown of thorns, enlarge thyself, that I too may place thee on my head! O nails, leave those innocent hands of my Lord, and come and pierce my heart with compassion and with love! For Thou, my Jesus, didst die, as St. Paul says, to gain dominion over the living and the dead, not by means of chastisements, but by love:" For to this end Christ died and rose again: that He might be Lord both of the dead and of the living.[28]

"O robber of hearts, the strength of Thy love has broken the exceeding hardness of our hearts! Thou hast inflamed the whole world with Thy love. O most loving Lord, inebriate our hearts with this wine, consume them with this fire, pierce them with this dart of Thy love! Thy Cross is indeed an arrow which pierces hearts. May all the world know that my heart is smitten! O sweetest love, what hast Thou done? Thou hast come to heal me, and Thou hast wounded me. Thou hast come to teach me, and Thou hast made me well-nigh mad. O madness full of wisdom, may I never live without you! All, O Lord, that I behold upon the cross invites me to love Thee: the wood, the figure, the wounds of Thy body; and above all, Thy love, engages me to love Thee, and never to forget Thee more."[29]

But in order to arrive at the perfect love of Jesus Christ, we must adopt the means. Behold, then, the means which St. Thomas Aquinas gives us:[30]

1. To have a constant remembrance of the benefits of God, both general and particular.
2. To consider the infinite goodness of God, who is ever waiting to do us good, and who ever loves us, and seeks from us our love.
3. To avoid even the smallest thing that could offend him.
4. To renounce all the sensible goods of this world, riches, honors, and sensual pleasures.

Father Tauler[31] says that meditation on the sacred Passion of Jesus Christ is a great means also for acquiring his perfect love.

Who can deny that, of all devotions, devotion to the Passion of Jesus Christ is the most useful, the most tender, the most agreeable to God, one that gives the greatest consolation to sinners, and at the same time most powerfully enkindles loving souls? Whence is it that we receive so many blessings, if it be not from the Passion of Jesus Christ? Whence have we hope of pardon, courage against temptations, confidence that we shall go to heaven? Whence are so many lights to know the truth, so many loving calls, so many spurring to change our life, so many desires to give ourselves up to God, except from the Passion of Jesus Christ? The Apostle therefore had but too great reason to declare him to be excommunicated who did not love Jesus Christ. If any man loves not our Lord Jesus Christ, let him be anathema.[32]

St. Bonaventure says there is no devotion more fitted for sanctifying a soul than meditation on the Passion of Jesus Christ; whence he advises us to meditate every day upon the Passion if we would advance in the love of God. "If you would make progress, meditate daily on the Passion of the Lord; for nothing works such an entire sanctification in the soul, as the meditation of the Passion of Christ."[33] And before him St. Augustine, as

Bustis relates, said, that one tear shed in memory of the Passion is worth more than to fast weekly on bread and water fora year.[34] Wherefore the saints were always occupied in considering the sorrows of Jesus Christ: it was by this means that St. Francis of Assisi became a seraph. He was one day found by a gentleman shedding tears and crying out with a loud voice: being asked the cause "I weep," he answered, "over the sorrows and ignominies of my Lord: and what causes me the greatest sorrow is, that men, for whom he suffered so much, live in forgetfulness of him." And on saying this he wept the more, so that this gentleman also began to weep. When the saint heard the bleating of a lamb or saw anything which reminded him of the Passion of Jesus, he immediately shed tears. On another occasion, being sick, someone told him to read some pious book. "My book," he replied, "is Jesus crucified." Hence, he did nothing but exhort his brethren to be ever thinking of the Passion of Jesus Christ. Tiepoli writes: "He who becomes not inflamed with the love of God by looking on Jesus dead upon the cross, will never love at all."

Affections and Prayers.

O Eternal Word! Thou hast spent three-and-thirty years in labors and fatigues; Thou hast given Thy life and Thy blood for man's salvation; in short, Thou hast spared nothing to make men love Thee; and how is it possible that there should be those who know this, and yet do not love Thee? O God, amongst these ungrateful ones I also may be numbered! I see the wrong I have done Thee; O my Jesus, have pity upon me! I offer Thee this ungrateful heart—ungrateful it is true, but penitent. Yes, I repent above every other evil, O my dear Redeemer, for having despised Thee! I repent, and I am sorry with my whole heart. O my soul, love a God who is bound like a criminal for thee; a God scourged like a slave for thee; a God made a mock-king for thee; a God, in short, dead upon a cross, as the vilest outcast for thee! Yes, my Savior, my God, I love Thee, I love Thee! Bring continually to my remembrance, I beseech Thee, all that Thou hast suffered for me, so that I may never more forget to love Thee. O cords that bound my Jesus, bind me to Jesus; thorns that crowned my Jesus, pierce me with the love of Jesus; nails that transfixed my Jesus, nail me to the Cross of Jesus, that I may live and die united to Jesus. O blood of Jesus, inebriate me with his holy love! O death of Jesus, make me die to every earthly affection! Pierced feet of my Lord, I embrace you; deliver me from hell, which I have deserved; my Jesus, in hell I could no more love Thee, and yet I desire to love Thee always. Save me, my dearest Savior; bind me to Thyself, that I may never again lose Thee. O Mary, refuge of sinners, and Mother of my Savior! help a sinner who wishes to love God, and who recommends himself to thee; succor me for the love thou barest to Jesus Christ.

II.

How much Jesus Christ deserves to be Loved by us, on Account of the Love He has shown us in Instituting the most Holy Sacrament of the Altar.

Jesus, knowing that His hour was come, that He should pass out of this world to the Father: having loved His own ... He loved them unto the end.[35] Our most loving Savior, knowing that his hour had now come for leaving this earth, desired, before he went to die for us, to leave us the greatest possible mark of his love; and this was the gift of the most Holy Sacrament.

St. Bernardine of Sienna remarks, that men remember more continually and love more tenderly the signs of love which are shown to them in the hour of death.[36] Hence it is the custom that friends, when about to die, leave to those persons whom they have loved some gift, such as a garment or a ring, as a memorial of their affection. But what hast Thou, O my Jesus, left us, when quitting this world, in memory of Thy love? Not, indeed, a garment or a ring, but Thine own body, Thy blood, Thy soul, Thy divinity, Thy whole self, without reserve. "He gave thee all," says St. John Chrysostom; "He left nothing for himself."[37]

The Council of Trent says,[38] that in this gift of the Eucharist Jesus Christ desired, as it were, to pour forth all the riches of the love he had for men. And the Apostle observes, that Jesus desired to bestow this gift upon men on the very night itself when they were planning his death: The same night in which He was betrayed, He took bread; and giving thanks, broke and said: Take ye, and eat: this is My body.[39] St. Bernardine of Sienna says, that Jesus Christ, burning with love for us, and not content with being prepared to give his life for us, was constrained by the excess of his love to work a greater work before he died; and this was to give his own body for our food.[40]

This Sacrament, therefore, was rightly named by St. Thomas, "the Sacrament of love, the pledge of love."[41] Sacrament of love; for love was the only motive which induced Jesus

Christ to give us in it his whole self, Pledge of love; so that if we had ever doubted his love, we should have in this sacrament a pledge of it: as if our Redeemer, in leaving us this gift, had said: O souls, if you ever doubt my love, behold, I leave you myself in this Sacrament: with such a pledge, you can never any more doubt that I love you, and love you to excess. But more, St. Bernard calls this sacrament "the love of loves;"[42] because this gift comprehends all the other gifts bestowed upon us by our Lord, creation, redemption, predestination to glory; so that the Eucharist is not only a pledge of the love of Jesus Christ, but of paradise, which he desires also to give us. "In which, "says the Church, "a pledge of future glory is given us."[43] Hence St. Philip Neri could find no other name for Jesus Christ in the Sacrament save that of "love;" and so, when the holy Viaticum was brought to him, he was heard to exclaim, "Behold my love; give me my love."

The prophet Isaias [44] desired that the whole world should know the tender inventions that our God has made use of, wherewith to make men love him. And who could ever have thought if he himself had not done it that the Incarnate Word would hide himself under the appearances of bread, to become himself our food? "Does it not seem folly," says St. Augustine, "to say, Eat my flesh; drink my blood?"[45] When Jesus Christ revealed to his disciples the sacrament he desired to leave them, they could not bring themselves to believe him; and they left him, saying: How can this Man give us His flesh to eat? ... This saying is hard, and who can hear it?[46] But that which men could neither conceive nor believe, the great love of Jesus Christ hath thought of and accomplished. Take ye, and eat, said he to his disciples before he went to die; and through them to us all. Receive and eat: but what food shall that be, O Savior of the world, which Thou desire to give us before Thou die? Take ye and eat; this is my body.[47] This is not earthly food; it is I who give myself entirely to you.

And oh, with what desire does Jesus Christ pant to come into our souls in the Holy Communion! With desire I have desired to eat this pasch with you before I suffer.[48] So he spoke on that night in which he instituted this sacrament of love. With desire I have desired: so did the excessive love which he bore us cause him to speak, as St. Laurence Justinian remarks: "These are the words of most burning love."[49] And in order that everyone might easily receive him, he desired to leave himself under the appearance of bread; for if he had left himself under the appearance of some rare or very costly food, the poor would have been deprived of him; but no, Jesus would hide himself under the form of bread, which costs but little, and can be found everywhere, in order that all in every country might be able to find him and receive him.

In order, then, to excite us to receive him in the Holy Communion, he not only exhorts us to do so by so many invitations,—Come, eat My bread; and drink the wine which I have mingled for you;[50] Eat, O friends, and drink,[51] speaking of this heavenly bread and wine, but he even gives us a formal precept: Take ye, and eat; this is My body. And more than this; that we may go and receive him, he entices us with the promise of paradise. He that eats My flesh hath everlasting life. He that eats this bread shall live forever.[52] And still more, he threatens us with hell, and exclusion from paradise, if we refuse to communicate. Except you eat the flesh of the Son of Man, you shall not have life in you.[53] These invitations, these promises, these threats, all proceed from the great desire he must come to us in this sacrament.

But why is it that Jesus Christ so desires that we should receive him in the Holy Communion? Here is the reason. St. Denis says that love always sighs after and tends to union, and so also says St. Thomas, "Lover's desire of two to become one."[54] Friends who really love each other would like to be so united as to become one person. Now this is what the infinite love of God for man has done; that he would not only give us himself in the eternal kingdom, but even in this life would permit men to possess him in the most intimate union, by giving them himself, whole and entire, under the appearances of bread in the sacrament. He stands there as though behind a wall; and from thence he beholds, as it were, through a closed lattice: Behold He stands behind our wall, looking through the windows, looking through the lattices.[55] It is true, we do not see him; but he sees us, and is there really present: he is present, in order that we may possess him: but he hides himself from us to make us desire him: and as long as we have not reached our true country, Jesus desires to give himself wholly to us, and to remain united with us.

He could not satisfy his love by giving himself to the human race by his Incarnation and by his Passion, dying for all men upon the cross; but he desired to find out a way whereby he might give himself entirely to each one of us in particular; and for this end he instituted the Sacrament of the Altar, in order to unite himself wholly to each: He that eats My flesh, he said, abide in me and I in him.[56] In Holy Communion Jesus unites himself to the soul, and the soul to Jesus; and this is not a union of mere affection, but it is a true and real union. Hence St. Francis de Sales says: "In no other action can the Savior be considered more tender or more loving than in this, in which he annihilates himself, so to say, and reduces himself to food, in order to penetrate our souls, and to unite himself to the hearts of his faithful."[57] St. John Chrysostom says, that Jesus Christ, through the ardent love which he bore us, desired so to unite himself to us, as to become one and the same thing with us. "He mingled himself with us, that we might be one thing; for this is the property of those who ardently love."[58]

"It was Thy wish, in short," says St. Laurence Justinian, "O God, enamored of our souls, to make, by means of this sacrament, Thine own heart, by an inseparable union, one and the same heart with ours!"[59] St. Bernardine of Sienna adds, that "the gift of Jesus Christ to us as our food was the last step of his love; since he gives himself to us in order to unite himself wholly to us; in the same way as food becomes united with him who partakes of it."[60] Oh, how delighted is Jesus Christ to be united with our souls! He one day said to his beloved servant, Margaret of Ypres, after Communion, "See, my daughter, the beautiful union that exists between me and thee: come, then, love me; and let us remain ever united in love, and let us never separate again."

We must, then, be persuaded that a soul can neither do, nor think of doing, anything which gives greater pleasure to Jesus Christ than to communicate frequently, with dispositions suitable to the great guest whom she must receive into her heart. I have said suitable, not indeed worthy dispositions; for if worthy were necessary, who could ever communicate? Another God would alone be worthy to receive God. By suitable, I mean such dispositions as become a miserable creature, clothed with the unhappy flesh of Adam. Ordinarily speaking, it is sufficient if a person communicates in a state of grace, and with a great desire of growing in the love of Jesus Christ. St. Francis de Sales said, "It is by love alone that we must receive Jesus Christ in the Communion, since it is through love alone that he gives himself to us."[61] For the rest, with regard to the number of times a person should communicate, in this he should be guided by the advice of his spiritual Father. Nevertheless, we should be aware that no state of life or employment, neither the married state nor business, prevents frequent Communion, when the director thinks it advisable, as Pope Innocent XI. has declared in his decree of 1679, when he says, "Frequent Communion must be left to the judgment of the confessors ... who, for lay persons in business, or in the marriage state, must recommend it according as they see it will be profitable for their salvation."[62]

We must next understand that there is nothing from which we can derive such profit as from Communion. The Eternal Father has made Jesus Christ the possessor of all his own heavenly treasures. The Father hath given all things into His hands.[63] Hence, when Jesus Christ comes to a soul in Holy Communion, he brings with him boundless treasures of grace; and consequently after Communion we can justly say, Now all good things came to me together with it.[64] St. Denis says, that the Sacrament of the Eucharist is far more powerful for the sanctification of souls than all other spiritual means of grace;[65] and St. Vincent Ferrer, that one Communion does more for the soul than a week's fasting on bread and water.

In the first place, as the Council of Trent teaches, Communion is that great remedy which frees us from venial and preserves us against mortal sins.[66] It is said "from daily faults;" because according to St. Thomas,[67] a man is excited by means of this sacrament to make acts of love, by which venial sins are forgiven. And it is said that "we are preserved from mortal sins, because Communion increases grace, which will preserve us from great faults." Hence Innocent III. says, that Jesus Christ delivered us from the power of sin by his Passion, but that by the Eucharist he delivers us from the power of sinning.[68]

This Sacrament, moreover, above all others, inflames our souls with divine love. God is love.[69] And he is a fire which consumes all earthly affections in our hearts. He is a consuming fire.[70] And for this very purpose, namely, to enkindle this fire, the Son of God came upon earth. I am come to send fire on the earth; and he added that he desired nothing but to see this fire enkindled in our souls: And what will I but that it be kindled?[71] And oh, what flames of love does not Jesus Christ light up in the heart of everyone who receives him devoutly in this sacrament! St. Catharine of Sienna once saw the Host in a priest's hand appearing as a globe of fire; and the saint was astonished that the hearts of all men were not burned up, and, as it were, reduced to ashes by such a flame. Such brilliant rays issued from the face of St. Rose of Lima after Communion, as to dazzle the eyes of those who saw her; and the heat from her mouth was so intense, that a hand held near it was scorched. It is related of St. Wenceslaus, that by merely visiting the churches where the Blessed Sacrament was kept, he was inflamed by such an ardor, that his servant who accompanied him did not feel the cold, if when walking on the snow he trod in the footsteps of the saint.

St. John Chrysostom says that the most Holy Sacrament is a burning fire; so that when we leave the altar we breathe forth flames of love, which make us objects of terror to hell.[72] The spouse of the Canticles says: He brought me into the cellar of wine, He set in order charity in me.[73] St. Gregory of Nyssa says that Communion is precisely this cellar of wine, in which the soul becomes so inebriated with divine love, that it forgets and loses sight of creatures; and this is that languishing with love of which the spouse again speaks: Stay me up with flowers, compass me about with apples, because I languish with love.[74]

Someone will say: "But this is the very reason why I do not communicate frequently, because I see that I am so cold in the love of God." Gerson answers such a one by saying: "Do you, therefore, because you are cold, willingly keep away from the fire? Rather, because you feel yourself cold, should you so much the more frequently approach this sacrament, if you really desire to love Jesus Christ." "Although it be with lukewarmness," wrote St. Bonaventure, "still approach, trusting in the mercy of God. The more one feels himself sick, the greater need has he of a physician."[75] In like manner, St. Francis de Sales: "Two sorts of persons ought to go frequently to Communion: the perfect, in order to remain so; and the imperfect, in order to be become perfect."[76] But for frequent Communion, it is at least necessary to have a great desire to become a saint and to grow in the love of Jesus Christ. Our Lord said once to St. Matilda: "When you go to Communion desire all the love which a soul has ever had for me, and I will receive your love according to your desire."[77]

Affections and Prayers.

God of love, O infinite lover, worthy of infinite love, tell me what more canst Thou invent to make us love Thee? It was not sufficient for Thee to become man, and to subject Thyself to all our miseries; not sufficient to shed all Thy blood for us in torments, and then to die overwhelmed with sorrow, upon a cross destined for the most shameful malefactors. Thou didst, at last, oblige Thyself to be hidden under the species of bread and wine, to become our food, and so united with each one of us. Tell me, I repeat, what more canst Thou invent to make Thyself loved by us? Ah, wretched shall we be if we do not love Thee in this life! And when we shall have entered eternity, what remorse shall we not feel for not having loved Thee! My Jesus, I will not die without loving Thee, and loving Thee exceedingly! I am heartily sorry and am pained for having so greatly offended Thee. But now I love Thee above all things. I love Thee more than myself, and I consecrate to Thee all my affections. Do Thou, who inspires! me with this desire, give me also grace to accomplish it. My Jesus, my Jesus, I desire nothing of Thee but Thyself. Now that Thou hast drawn me to Thy love, I leave all, I renounce all, and I bind myself to Thee: Thou alone art sufficient for me. Mary, Mother of God, pray to Jesus for me, and make me a saint! Add this also to the many wonders thou hast done in changing sinners into saints.

III.

The Great Confidence we ought to have in the Love which Jesus Christ has shown us and in all He has done for us.

David placed all his hope of salvation in his future Redeemer, and said: Into Thy hands, O Lord, I commend my spirit; Thou hast redeemed me, O Lord, the God of truth.

But how much more ought we to place our confidence in Jesus Christ, now that he has come, and has accomplished the work of redemption! Hence each one of us should say and repeat again and again with greater confidence: Into Thy hands, O Lord, I commend my spirit; Thou hast redeemed me, O Lord, the God of truth.[78]

If we have great reason to fear everlasting death on account of our sins against God, we have, on the other hand, far greater reason to hope for everlasting life through the merits of Jesus Christ, which are infinitely more powerful for our salvation than our sins are for our damnation. We have sinned and have deserved hell; but the Redeemer has come to take upon himself all our offences, and to make satisfaction for them by His sufferings: Surely, He hath borne our infirmities, and carried our sorrows.[79]

In the same unhappy moment in which we sinned; God had already written against us the sentence of eternal death; but what has our merciful Redeemer done? Blotting out the handwriting of the decree which was against us, ... the same He took out of the way, fastening it to the cross.[80] He cancelled by his blood the decree of our condemnation, and then fastened it to the cross, in order that, when we look at the sentence of our damnation for the sins we have committed, we may at the same time see the cross on which Jesus Christ died and blotted out this sentence by his blood, and so regain hope of pardon and everlasting life.

Oh, how far more powerfully does the blood of Jesus Christ speak for us, and obtain mercy for us from God, than did the blood of Abel speak against Cain! You are come to Jesus the mediator of the New Testament, and to the sprinkling of blood, which speaks better than that of Abel.[81] As if the Apostle had said, "O sinners, happy are you to be able, after you have sinned, to have re course to Jesus crucified, who has shed all his blood, in order to become the mediator of peace between sinners and God, and to obtain pardon for them! Your iniquities cry out against you, but the blood of the Redeemer pleads in your favor; and the divine justice cannot but be appeased by the voice of this precious blood."

It is true that we shall have to render a rigorous account to the Eternal Judge of all our sins. But who is to be our Judge? The Father hath committed all judgment to the Son.[82] Let us comfort ourselves, the Eternal Father has committed our judgment to our own Redeemer. Therefore St. Paul encourages us, saying, Who is he that shall condemn? Christ Jesus who died, ... who also maketh intercession for us.[83] Who is the judge to condemn us? It is that same Savior who, in order not to condemn us to everlasting death, vouchsafed himself to be condemned and to die; and not content with this, at this moment intercedes with his Father for our salvation. Hence St. Thomas of Villanova says: "What do you fear, O sinner, if you detest your sin? How will he condemn you, who died in order not to condemn you? how will he cast you from him, if you return to his feet, he who came from heaven to seek you at the very time you were flying from him?"[84]

And if we fear on account of our frailty to fall under the assaults of our enemies, against whom we must continually wage war, behold what we have to do, as the Apostle ad-monishes us: Let us run to the fight proposed unto us: looking on Jesus the author and finisher of faith, who having joy proposed unto Him, underwent the cross, despising the shame.[85] Let us go out to the battle with great courage, looking at Jesus crucified, who from his cross offers us his assistance, the victory, and crown. In past times we fell into sin because we left off looking at the wounds and the pains endured by our Redeemer, and so we did not have recourse to him for help. But if for the future we set before our eyes all he has suffered for love of us, and how he ever stands ready to assist us when we have recourse to him, it is certain that we shall not be conquered by our enemies. St. Teresa said, with her wonted generosity, "I do not understand the fears of certain persons, who say, The devil, the devil, so long as we can say, God, God, and make Satan tremble."[86] On the other hand, the saint assures us, that if we do not place all our confidence in God, all our own exertions will be of little or no avail. "All our exertions," these are her own words, "are of little use, if we do not give up entirely all trust in ourselves, and place it altogether in God."[87] Oh, what two great mysteries of hope and love for us are the

Passion of Jesus Christ and the Sacrament of the Altar!—mysteries, which we could have never believed, had not faith assured us of them. That God Almighty should deign to become man, shed all his blood, and die of sorrow upon a cross, and why? To pay for our sins, and gain salvation for us rebellious worms! And then his own very body, once sacrificed upon the Cross for us, this he vouchsafes to give us for our food, in order to become wholly united with us! O God, how should not these two mysteries consume with love the hearts of all men! And what sinner is there, be he ever so abandoned, who can despair of pardon, if he repents of the evil he has done, when he sees a God so full of love for men, and so inclined to do them good? Hence St. Bonaventure, full of confidence, said, "I will have great confidence, firmly hoping that he who has done and suffered so much for my salvation will deny me nothing that I have need of."[88] How can he refuse to give me the graces necessary for my salvation, who has done and suffered so much to save me?

Let us go therefore (the Apostle exhorts us) with confidence to the throne of grace, that we may obtain mercy, and find grace in seasonable aid.[89] The throne of grace is the cross on which Jesus sits to dispense graces and mercy to all who come to him. But we must quickly have recourse to him, if we would find seasonable aid for our salvation: for there will come a time perhaps when we shall no longer be able to find it. Let us go quickly then and embrace the cross of Jesus Christ and let us go with great confidence. Let us not be frightened by the sight of our miseries; in Jesus crucified we shall find all riches, all grace: In all things you are made rich in Him, ... so that nothing is wanting to you in any grace.[90] The merits of Jesus Christ have enriched us with all the divine treasures, and have made us capable of every grace we can desire.

St. Leo says, "that Jesus has brought us by his death better than the devil has done us harm by sin."[91] And by these words he explains what St. Paul said before him, that the gift of redemption is greater than sin: grace has overcome the offence. Not as the offence, so also is the gift: where sin abounded, grace hath abounded more.[92] From this the Savior encourages us to hope for every favor and every grace through his merits. And see how he teaches us the way to obtain all we want from his Eternal Father: Amen, amen, I say to you, if you ask the Father anything in My name, He will give it you.[93] Whatever you desire, he says, ask for it of the Father in my name, and I promise you that you shall be heard. And indeed, how shall the Father be able to deny us, when he has given us his only-begotten Son, whom he loves as himself? He that spared not even His own Son, but delivered Him up for us all, how hath He not also, with Him, given us all things?[94] The Apostle says all things; so that no grace is excepted, neither pardon, nor perseverance, nor holy love, nor perfection, nor paradise, "all, all, he has given us." But we must pray to him. God is all liberality to those who call upon him: Rich unto all that call upon Him.[95]

I will again quote here many other beautiful thoughts of the Venerable John of Avila, which he has left us in his letters, on the great confidence we should have in the merits of Jesus Christ:

"Do not forget that Jesus Christ is the mediator between the Eternal Father and ourselves; and that we are beloved by him, and united to him by so strong bonds of love that nothing can break them, so long as a man does not himself dissolve them by some mortal sin. The blood of Jesus cries out and asks mercy for us; and cries out so loudly that the noise of our sins is not heard. The death of Jesus Christ hath put to death our sins: O Death, I will be thy death![96] Those who are lost are not lost for want of means of satisfaction, but because they would not avail themselves of the sacraments as the means of profiting by the satisfaction made by Jesus Christ.

"Jesus has taken upon himself the affair of remedying our evils, as if it had been personally his own affair. So that he has called our sins his own, although he did not commit them, and has sought pardon for them; and with the most tender love has prayed, as if he were praying for himself, that all who should have recourse to him might become objects of love. And as he sought, so he found, because God has so ordained that Jesus and ourselves should be so united in one, that either he and we should be loved, or he and we hated: and since Jesus is not or cannot be hated, in the same way, if we remain united by love to Jesus, we shall be also loved. By his being loved by God, we are also loved, seeing that Jesus Christ can do more to make us loved than we can do to make ourselves hated; since the Eternal Father loves Jesus Christ far more than he hates sinners.

"Jesus said to his Father: Father, I will that where I am, they also whom Thou hast given Me may be with Me.[97] Love has conquered hatred; and thus we have been pardoned and loved, and are secure of never being abandoned, so strong is the tie of love that binds us. The Lord said by Isaias: Can a woman forget her infant? And if she should forget, yet will I not forget thee. Behold, I have graven Thee in My hands.[98] He has graven us in his hands with his own blood. Thus, we should not trouble ourselves about anything, since everything is ordained by those hands which were nailed to the cross in testimony of the love he bears us.

"Nothing can so trouble us on which Jesus Christ cannot reassure us. Let the sins I have committed surround me, let the devils lay snares for me, let fears for the future accuse me, by demanding mercy of the most tender Jesus Christ, who has loved me even until death, I cannot possibly lose confidence; for I see myself so highly valued, that God gave himself for me. O my Jesus, sure haven for those who seek Thee in time of peril! O most watchful Pastor, he deceives himself who does not trust in Thee, if only he has the will to amend his life! Therefore, Thou hast said: I am here, fear not; I am he who afflicts and who consoles. Some from time to time I place in desolations, which seem equal to hell itself; but after a while I bring them out and con sole them. I am thine advocate, who have made thy cause my own. I am thy surety, who am come to pay thy debts. I am thy Lord, who has redeemed thee with my blood, not in order to abandon thee, but to enrich thee, having bought thee at a great price. How shall I fly from him who seeks me, when I went forth to meet those who sought to outrage me? I did not turn away my face from him who struck me; and shall I from him who would adore me? How can my children doubt that I love them, seeing that out of love to them I placed myself in the hands of my enemies? Whom have I ever despised that loved me? Whom have I ever abandoned that sought my aid? Even I go seeking those that do not seek me."[99]

If you believe that the Eternal Father has given you his Son, believe also that he will give you everything else which is infinitely less than his Son. Do not think that Jesus Christ is forgetful of you, since he has left you, as the greatest memorial and pledge of his love, himself in the Most Holy Sacrament of the Altar.

Affections and Prayers.

O my Jesus, my love, what joyful hope does Thy Passion give me! How can I possibly fear not to receive from an Almighty God who has given me all his blood, the pardon of my sins, paradise, and all other graces that I require! Ah, my Jesus, my hope and my love, Thou, in order that I might not perish, didst give Thy life; I love Thee above every good, my Redeemer and my God. Thou gavest Thyself entirely to me; I give Thee my whole will, and with it I repeat that I love Thee, and I will always say, I love Thee, I love Thee. So I always desire to say in this life so I wish to die, breathing forth my last sigh with this dear word on my lips, My God, I love Thee; and from that moment I may commence a love towards Thee which shall last forever, and without cessation for all eternity. I love Thee, then; and because I love Thee, I repent above all things for having offended Thee. In order not to lose a passing satisfaction, I have been willing, wretch that I am, to lose Thee so often, O infinite good! This thought torments me more than any pain: but it is a consolation to me to think that I have to do with infinite goodness, that knows not how to despise a heart that truly loves. Oh, that I could die for Thee, who didst die for me! My dear Redeemer, I surely hope of Thee eternal salvation in the life to come, and in this life I hope for holy perseverance in Thy love; and therefore I propose always to ask it of Thee. And do Thou, by the merits of Thy death, give me perseverance in praying to Thee. This too I ask and hope of thee, O Mary my Queen!

IV.

How much we are obliged to love Jesus Christ.

Jesus Christ as God has a claim on all our love; but by the love which he has shown us, he wished to put us, so to speak, under the necessity of loving him, at least in gratitude for all that he has done and suffered for us. He has greatly loved us, that we might love him greatly. "Why does God love us, but that he may be loved?"[100] wrote St. Bernard. And Moses had said the same before him: And now, Israel, what doth the Lord thy God require of thee, but that thou fear the Lord thy God ... and love Him?[101] Therefore the first command which he gave us was this; Thou shalt love the Lord thy God with Thy whole heart.[102] And St. Paul says, that love is the fulfilling of the law: Love is the fulfilling of the law.[103] For "fulfilling" the Greek text has the "embracing of the law;"[104] love embraces the entire law.

Who, indeed, at the sight of a crucified God dying for our love can refuse to love him? Those thorns, those nails, that cross, those wounds, and that blood, call upon us, and irresistibly urge us, to love him who has loved us so much. One heart is too little wherewith to Jove this God so enamored of us. To requite the love of Jesus Christ, it would require another God to die for his love. "Ah, why," exclaims St. Francis de Sales, "do we not throw ourselves on Jesus Christ, to die on the cross with him who was pleased to die there for the love of us?"[105] The Apostle clearly impresses on us that Jesus Christ died for us for this end, that we might no longer live for ourselves, but solely for that God who died for us: Christ died for all, that they also who lire may not now live to themselves, but unto Him who died for them.[106]

And the recommendation of Ecclesiasticus is here in point: Forget not the kindness of thy surety; for He hath given His life for thee.[107] Be not unmindful of him who has stood surety for thee; who, to satisfy for thy sins, was willing to pay off, by his death, the debt of punishment due from thee. Oh, how desirous is Jesus Christ that we should continually remember his Passion! and how it saddens him to see that we are so unmindful of it! Should a person endure one of his friend's affronts, blows, and imprisonment, how afflicting would it be for him to know that that friend afterwards never gave it a thought and cared not even to hear it spoken of! On the contrary, how gratified would he be to know that his friend constantly spoke of it with the warmest gratitude, and often thanked him for it. So it is pleasing to Jesus Christ when we preserve in our minds a grateful and loving recollection of the sorrows and death which he underwent for us. Jesus Christ was the desire of all the ancient Fathers; he was the desire of all nations before he was yet come upon earth. Now, how much more ought he to be our only desire and our only love, now that we know that he is really come, and are aware how much he has done and suffered for us, so that he even died upon the cross for love of us!

For this purpose, he instituted the Sacrament of the Holy Eucharist on the day preceding his death, and gave us the injunction, that as often as we should be nourished with his most sacred flesh, we should be mindful of his death: Take ye and eat; this is My body. ... This do for a commemoration of Me, etc. For as often as you shall eat this bread and drink the chalice, you shall show the death of the Lord until He come.[108] Wherefore the holy Church prays: "O God! who under this wonderful Sacrament hast left us a memorial of Thy Passion,"[109] etc. And she also sings: "O sacred banquet, in which Christ is taken, the memory of his Passion is renewed,"[110] etc. Hence, we may gather how pleasing to Jesus Christ are they who think frequently of his Passion, since it was for this very purpose that he left himself in the holy Sacrament upon our altars, in order that we might bear in continual and grateful remembrance all that he suffered for us, and by this means evermore increase our love towards him. St. Francis de Sales called Mount Calvary "the mountain of lovers." It is impossible to remember that mount and not love Jesus Christ, who died there for love of us.

O God! and how is it that men do not love this God who has done so much to be loved by men! Before the Incarnation of the Word, man might have doubted whether God loved him with a true love; but after the coming of the Son of God, and after his dying for the love of men, how can we possibly doubt of his love? "O man," says St. Thomas of Villanova, "look on that cross, on those torments, and that cruel death, which Jesus Christ has suffered for thee: after so great and so many tokens of his love, thou canst no longer entertain a doubt that he loves thee and loves thee exceedingly." And St. Bernard says, that "the cross and every wound of our Blessed Redeemer cry aloud to make us understand the love he bears us."[111]

In this grand mystery of man's redemption, we must consider how Jesus employed all his thoughts and zeal to discover every means of making himself loved by us. Had he merely wished to die for our salvation, it would have been sufficient had he been slain by Herod with the other children; but no, he chose before dying to lead, during thirty-three years, a life of hardship and suffering; and during that time, with a view to win our love, he appeared in several different guises. First, as a poor child born in a stable; then as a little boy helping in the workshop; and finally, as a criminal executed on a cross. But before dying on the cross, we see him in many different states, one and all calculated to excite our compassion, and to make himself loved: in agony in the garden, bathed from head to foot in a sweat of blood; afterwards, in the court of Pilate, torn with scourges; then treated as a mock-king, with a reed in his hand, a ragged garment of purple on his shoulders, and a crown of thorns on his head; then dragged publicly through the streets to death, with the cross upon his shoulders; and at length, on the hill of Calvary, suspended on the cross by three iron nails. Tell me, does he merit our love or not, this God who has vouchsafed to endure all these torments, and to use so many means in order to captivate our love? Father John Rigouleux used to say: "I would spend my life in weeping for love of a God whose love induced him to die for the salvation of men."

"Love is a great thing,"[112] says St. Bernard. A great thing, a precious thing is love. Solomon, speaking of the divine wisdom, which is holy charity, called it an infinite treasure; because he that possesses charity is made partaker of the friendship of God: For she is an infinite treasure to men, which they that use become the friends of God.[113]

The angelic Doctor, St. Thomas, says, that charity is not only the queen of all virtues, but that, wherever she reigns, she draws along with her, as it were, in her train, all other virtues, and directs them all to bring us in closer union with God; but charity is properly that which unites us with God. As St. Bernard tells us: "Charity is a virtue uniting us with God."[114] And, indeed, it is over and over again signified in the holy Scriptures, that God loves whoever loves him: I love them that love Me. [115] If anyone loves me ... My Father will love Him; and We will come to him and will make Our abode with him.[116] He that abide in charity abide in God, and God in him.[117] Behold the beautiful union which charity produces; it unites the soul to God. Moreover, love supplies strength to practice and to suffer everything for God: Love is strong as death.[118] St. Augustine writes: "Nothing is so hard that cannot be subdued by the fire of love."[119] Wherefore the saint says, that where we love, either the labor is not felt, or if felt, the labor itself is loved: "In that which is loved, either there is no labor, or the labor is loved."[120]

Let us hear from St. John Chrysostom what are the effects of divine love in those souls in which it reigns: "When the love of God has taken possession of a soul, it produces an insatiable desire to work for the beloved; insomuch that however many and however vast the works which she does, and however prolonged the duration of her service, all seems nothing in her eyes, and she is afflicted at doing so little for God; and were it permitted her to die and consume herself for him, she would be most happy. Hence it is that she esteems herself an unprofitable servant in all that she does; because she is instructed by love to know what God deserves and sees by this clear light all the defects of her actions, and finds in them motives for confusion and pain, well aware how mean is all that she can do for so great a Lord."

"Oh! how those persons delude themselves," says St. Francis de Sales, "who place virtue in anything else but in loving God! Some," writes the saint, "put perfection in austerities, others in alms, others in prayer, others in frequenting the holy sacraments. For my part, I know of no other perfection than that of loving God with our whole heart; because all the other virtues, without love, are but a mere heap of stones. And if we do not perfectly enjoy this holy love, the fault lies with us, because we do not, once for all, come to the conclusion of giving up ourselves wholly to God."[121]

Our Lord said one day to St. Teresa, "Everything which does not give pleasure to me is vanity." Would that all understood well this great truth! For the rest, one thing is necessary.[122] It is not necessary to be rich in this world, to gain the esteem of others, to lead a life of ease, to enjoy dignities, to have a reputation for learning; it is only necessary to love God and to do his will. For this single end he has created us, for this he preserves our life; and thus, only can we gain admittance into Paradise. Put me as a seal upon thy heart, as a seal upon thy arm.[123] The Lord thus speaks to all his espoused souls. Put me as a seal upon thy heart and upon thine arm, in order that all thy desires and actions may tend to me; upon thy heart, that no other love but mine may enter there upon thine arm, in order that all thou dost may have me for its sole object. Oh, how quickly does that soul speed onwards to perfection, that in all its actions regards but Jesus crucified, and has no other pretension than to gratify him!

To acquire, then, a true love of Jesus Christ should be our only care. The masters of spiritual life describe the marks of true love. Love, say they, is fearful, and its fear is none other than that of displeasing God. It is generous, because, trusting in God, it is never daunted even at the greatest enterprises for his glory, it is strong, because it subdues all its evil appetites, even in the midst of the most violent temptations, and of the darkest desolations. It is obedient because it immediately flies to execute the divine will. It is pure, because it loves God alone, and for the sole reason that he deserves to be loved. It is ardent, because it would inflame all mankind, and willingly see them consumed with divine love. It is inebriating, for it causes the soul to live as it were out of itself, as if it no longer saw, nor felt, nor had any more senses left for earthly things, bent wholly on loving God. It is unitive, by producing a strict union between the will of the creature and the will of the Creator. It is longing, for it fills the soul with desires of leaving this world, to fly and unite itself perfectly with God in its true and happy country, where it may love him with all its strength.

But no one teaches us so well the real characteristics and practice of charity as the great preacher of charity, St. Paul. In his first epistle to the Corinthians, he says, in the first place, that without charity man is nothing, and that nothing profits him: If I should have all faith, so that I could remove mountains, and have not charity, I am nothing, And if I should distribute all my goods to feed the poor, and if I should deliver my body to be burned, and have not charity, it profits me nothing.[124] So that even should a per son have faith strong enough to remove mountains, like St. Gregory Thaumaturgus, but had not charity, it would profit him nothing. Should he give all his goods to the poor, and even willingly suffer martyrdom, but remain void of charity,—should he do it, that is, for any other end than that of pleasing God, it would profit him nothing at all. Then St. Paul gives us the marks of true charity, and at the same time teaches us the practice of those virtues which are the daughters of charity; and he goes on to say: Charity is patient, is kind; charity envieth not, dealeth not perversely; is not puffed up, is not ambitious;

seeketh not her own; is not provoked to anger, thinketh no evil; rejoiceth not in iniquity, but rejoiceth with the truth; beareth all things, believeth all things, hopeth all things, endureth all things.[125]

Let us therefore, in the present book, proceed to consider these holy practices, that we may thus see if the love which we owe to Jesus Christ truly reigns within us; as likewise that we may understand in what virtues we should chiefly exercise ourselves, to persevere and advance in this holy love.

Affections and Prayers.

O most lovely and most loving Heart of Jesus, miserable is the heart which does not love Thee! O God, for the love of men Thou didst die on the cross, helpless, and forsaken, and how then can men live so forgetful of Thee? O love of God! O ingratitude of man! O men, O men! do but cast one look on the innocent Son of God, agonizing on the cross, and dying for you, to satisfy the divine justice for your sins, and by this means to allure you to love him. Observe how, at the same time, he prays to his eternal Father to forgive you. Behold him and love him. Ah, my Jesus, how small is the number of those that love Thee! Wretched too am I; for I also have lived so many years unmindful of Thee, and have grievously offended Thee, my beloved Redeemer! It is not so much the punishment I have deserved that makes me weep, as the love which Thou hast borne me. O sorrows of Jesus! O ignominies of Jesus! O wounds of Jesus! O death of Jesus! O love of Jesus! rest deeply engraved in my heart, and may your sweet recollection be forever fixed there, to wound me and inflame me continually with love. I love Thee, my Jesus; I love Thee, my sovereign good; I love Thee, my love and my all; I love Thee, and I will love Thee forever. Oh, suffer me never more to forsake Thee, never more to lose Thee! Make me entirely Thine; do so by the merits of Thy death. In this I firmly trust. And I have a great confidence also in thy intercession, O Mary, my Queen; make me love Jesus Christ and make me also love thee, my Mother and my hope!

1

— . —

CHARITY IS PATIENT

HE THAT LOVES JESUS CHRIST LOVES SUFFERINGS

This earth is the place for meriting, and therefore it is a place for suffering. Our true country, where God has prepared for us repose in everlasting joy, is paradise. We have but a short time to stay in this world; but in this short time, we have many labors to undergo: Man born of a woman, living for a short time, is filled with many miseries.[1] We must suffer, and all must suffer; be they just, or be they sinners, each one must carry his cross. He that carries it with patience is saved; he that carries it with impatience is lost. St. Augustine says, the same miseries send some to paradise and some to hell: "One and the same blow lifts the good to glory, and reduces the bad to ashes."[2] The same saint observes, that by the test of suffering the chaff in the Church of God is distinguished from the wheat: he that humbles himself under tribulations, and is resigned to the will of God, is wheat for paradise; he that grows haughty and is enraged, and so forsakes God, is chaff for hell.

On the day when the cause of our salvation shall be decided, our life must be found conformable to the life of Jesus Christ, if we would enjoy the happy sentence of the predestined: For whom He foreknew He also predestinated to be made conformable to the image of His Son.[3] This was the end for which the Eternal Word descended upon earth, to teach us, by his example, to carry with patience the cross which God sends us: Christ suffered for us (wrote St. Peter), leaving you an example, that you should follow His steps.[4] So that Jesus Christ suffered on purpose to encourage us to suffer. O God! what a life was that of Jesus Christ! A life of ignominy and pain. The Prophet calls our Redeemer despised, and the most abject of men, a man of sorrows.[5] A man held in contempt, and treated as the lowest, the vilest among men, a man of sorrows; yes, for the life of Jesus Christ was made up of hardships and afflictions.

Now, in the same manner as God has treated his beloved Son, so does he treat everyone whom he loves, and whom he receives for his son: For whom the Lord loveth He chastiseth; and He scourgeth every son whom He receiveth.[6] For this reason he one day said to St. Teresa: "Know that the souls dearest to my Father are those who are afflicted with the greatest sufferings."[7] Hence the saint said of all her troubles, that she would not exchange them for all the treasures in the world. She appeared after her death to a soul, and revealed to her that she enjoyed an immense reward in heaven, not so much for her good works, as for the sufferings which she cheerfully bore in this life for the love of God; and that if she could possibly entertain a wish to return upon earth, the only reason would be in order that she might suffer more for God.

He that loves God in suffering earns a double reward in paradise. St. Vincent of Paul [8] said that it was a great misfortune to be free from suffering in this life. And he added that a congregation or an individual that does not suffer, and is applauded by all the world, is not far from a fall. It was on this account that St. Francis of Assisi, on the day that he had suffered nothing for God, became afraid lest God had forgotten him. St. John Chrysostom [9] says, that when God endows a man with the grace of suffering, he gives him a greater grace than that of raising the dead to life; because in performing miracles man remains God's debtor, whereas in suffering, God makes himself the debtor of man. And he adds,[10] that whoever endures something for God, even had he no other gift than the strength to suffer for the God whom he loves, this would procure for him an immense reward. Wherefore he affirmed, that he considered St. Paul to have received a greater grace in being bound in chains for Jesus Christ, than in being rapt to the third heaven in ecstasy.

But patience has a perfect work.[11] The meaning of this is, that nothing is more pleasing to God than to see a soul suffering with patience all the crosses sent her by him. The effect of love is to liken the lover to the person loved. St. Francis de Sales said, "All the wounds of Christ are so many mouths, which preach to us that we must suffer for him. The science of the saints is to suffer constantly for Jesus; and in this way we shall soon become saints." A person that loves Jesus Christ is anxious to be treated like Jesus Christ, poor, persecuted, and despised. St. John beheld all the saints clothed in white, and with palms in their hands: Clothed with white robes, and palms in their hands.[12] The palm is the symbol of martyrs, and yet all the saints did not suffer martyrdom; why, then, do all the saints bear palms in their hands? St. Gregory replies, that all the saints have been martyrs either of the sword or of patience; so that, he adds, "we can be martyrs without the sword, if we keep patience."[13]

The merit of a soul that loves Jesus Christ consists in loving and in suffering. Hear what our Lord said to St. Teresa: "Think you, my child, that merit consists in enjoyment? No, it consists in suffering and in loving. Look at my life, wholly embittered with afflictions. Be assured, my child, that the more my Father loves any one, the more sufferings he sends him; they are the standard of his love. Look at my wounds; your torments will never reach so far. It is absurd to suppose that my Father favors with his friendship those who are strangers to suffering."[14] And for our consolation St. Teresa makes this remark: "God never sends a trial, but he forthwith rewards it with some favor."[15] One day Jesus Christ appeared to the blessed Baptista Varani,[16] and told her of three special favors which he is wont to bestow on cherished souls: the first is, not to sin; the second, which is greater, to perform good works; the third, and the greatest of all, to suffer for his love. So that St. Teresa [17] used to say, whenever anyone does something for God, the Almighty repays him with some trial And therefore the saints, on receiving tribulations, thanked God for them. St. Louis of France, referring to his captivity in Turkey, said: "I rejoice, and thank God more for the patience which he accorded me in the time of my imprisonment, than if he had made me master of the universe." And when St. Elizabeth, princess of Thuringia, after her husband's death, was banished with her son from the kingdom, and found herself homeless and abandoned by all, she went to a convent of the Franciscans, and there had the Te Deum sung in thanksgiving to God for the signal favor of being allowed to suffer for his love.

St. Joseph Calasanctius used to say, "All suffering is slight to gain heaven." And the Apostle had already said the same: The sufferings of this time are not worthy to be compared with the glory to come, that shall be revealed in us.[18]

It would be a great gain for us to endure all the torments of all the martyrs during our whole lives, in order to enjoy one single moment of the bliss of paradise; with what readiness, then, should we embrace our crosses, when we know that the sufferings of this transitory life will gain for us an everlasting beatitude! That which is at present momentary and light of our tribulation, worketh for us above measure exceedingly an eternal weight of glory.[19] St. Agapitus, while still a mere boy in years, was threatened by the tyrant to have his head covered with a red-hot helmet; on which he replied, "And what better fortune could possibly befall me, than to lose my head here, to have it crowned hereafter in heaven?" This made St. Francis exclaim:

"I look for such a meed of bliss, That all my pains seem happiness."

But whoever desires the crown of paradise must needs combat and suffer: If we suffer, we shall also reign.[20] We cannot get a reward without merit; and no merit is to be had without patience: He is not crowned, except he strives lawfully.[21] And the person that strives with the greatest patience shall have the greatest reward. Wonderful indeed! When the temporal goods of this world are in question, worldlings endeavor to procure as much as they can; but when it is a question of the goods of eternal life, they say, "It is enough if we get a little corner in heaven!" Such is not the language of the saints: they are satisfied with anything whatever in this life, nay more, they strip themselves of all earthly goods; but concerning eternal goods, they strive to obtain them in as large a measure as possible. I would ask which of the two act with more wisdom and prudence?

But even with regard to the present life, it is certain that he who suffers with most patience enjoys the greatest peace. It was a saying of St. Philip Neri,[22] that in this world there is no purgatory; it is either all paradise or all hell: he that patiently supports tribulations enjoys a paradise; he that does not do so, suffers a hell. Yes, for (as St. Teresa writes) he that embraces the crosses sent him by God feels them not. St. Francis de Sales, finding himself on one occasion beset on every side with tribulations, said, "For some time back the severe oppositions and secret contrarieties which have befallen me afford me so sweet a peace, that nothing can equal it; and they give me such an assurance that my soul will ere long be firmly united with God, that I can say with all truth that they are the sole ambition, the sole desire of my heart."[23] And indeed peace can never be found by one who leads an irregular life, but only by him who lives in union with God and with his blessed will. A certain missionary of a religious Order, while in the Indies, was one day standing to witness the execution of a person under sentence of death, and already on the scaffold: the criminal called the missionary to him, and said, "You must know, Father, that I was once a member of your Order; whilst I observed the rules I led a very happy life; but when, afterwards, I began to relax in the strict observance of them, I immediately experienced pain in everything; so much so, that I abandoned the religious life, and gave myself up to vice, which has finally reduced me to the melancholy pass in which you at present behold me." And in conclusion he said, "I tell you this, that my example may be a warning to others." The Venerable Father Louis da Ponte said, "Take the sweet things of this life for bitter, and the bitter for sweet; and so you will be in the constant enjoyment of peace. Yes, for though the sweet are pleasant to sense, they invariably leave behind them the bitterness of remorse of conscience, on account of the imperfect satisfaction which, for the most part, they afford; but the bitter, when taken with patience from the hand of God, become sweet, and dear to the souls who love him."

Let us be convinced that in this valley of tears true peace of heart cannot be found, except by him who endures and lovingly embraces sufferings to please Almighty God: this is the consequence of that corruption in which all are placed through the infection of sin. The condition of the saints on earth is to suffer and to love; the condition of the saints in heaven is to enjoy and to love. Father Paul Segneri the younger, in a letter which he wrote one of his penitents to encourage her to suffer, gave her the counsel to keep these words inscribed at the foot of her crucifix: "'Tis thus one loves." It is not simply by suffering, but by desiring to suffer for the love of Jesus Christ, that a soul gives the surest signs of really loving him. And what greater acquisition (said St. Teresa) can we possibly make than to have some token of gratifying Almighty God?[24] Alas, how ready are the greatest part of men to take alarm at the bare mention of crosses, of humiliations, and of afflictions! Nevertheless, there are many souls who find all their delight in suffering, and who would be quite disconsolate did they pass their time on this earth without suffering. The sight of Jesus crucified (said a devout person) renders the cross so lovely to me, that it seems to me I could never be happy without suffering; the love of Jesus Christ is sufficient for me for all. Listen how Jesus advises everyone who would follow him to take up and carry his cross: Let him take up his cross, and follow Me.[25] But we must take it up and carry it, not by constraint and against our will, but with humility, patience, and love.

Oh, how acceptable to God is he that humbly and patiently embraces the crosses which he sends him! St. Ignatius of Loyola said, "There is no wood so apt to enkindle and maintain love towards God as the wood of the cross;" that is, to love him in the midst of sufferings. One day St. Gertrude asked our Lord what she could offer him most acceptable, and he replied, "My child, thou canst do nothing more gratifying to me than to submit patiently to all the tribulations that befall thee." Wherefore the great servant of God, Sister Victoria Angelini, affirmed that one day of crucifixion was worth a hundred years of all other spiritual exercises. And the Venerable Father John of Avila said, "One 'blessed be God' in contrarieties is worth more than a thousand thanksgivings in prosperity." Alas, how little men know of the inestimable value of afflictions endured for God! The Blessed Angela of Foligno said, "that if we knew the just value of suffering for God, it would become an object of plunder;" which is as much as to say, that each one would seek an opportunity of robbing his neighbor of the occasions of suffering. For this reason, St. Mary Magdalene of Pazzi, well aware as she was of the merit of sufferings, sighed to have her life prolonged rather than to die and go to Heaven, "because," said she, " in Heaven one can suffer no more."

A soul that loves God has no other end in view but to be wholly united with him; but let us learn from St. Catharine of Genoa what is necessary to be done to arrive at this perfect union: "To attain union with God, adversities are indispensable, because by them God aims at destroying all our corrupt propensities within and without. And hence all injuries, contempt, infirmities, abandonment of relatives and friends, confusions, temptations, and other mortifications, all are in the highest degree necessary for us, in order that we may carry on the fight, until by repeated victories we come to extinguish within us all vicious movements, so that they are no longer felt; and we shall never arrive at divine union until adversities, instead of seeming bitter to us, become all sweet for God's sake."

It follows, then, that a soul that sincerely desires to belong to God must be resolved, as St. John of the Cross [26] writes, not to seek enjoyments in this life, but to suffer in all things; she must embrace with eagerness all voluntary mortifications, and with still greater eagerness those which are involuntary, since they are the more welcome to Almighty God.

The patient man is better than the valiant.[27] God is pleased with a person who practices mortification by fasting, haircloths, and disciplines, on account of the courage displayed in such mortifications; but he is much more pleased with those who have the courage to bear patiently and gladly such crosses as come from his own divine hand. St. Francis de Sales said, "Such mortifications as come to us from the hand of God, or from men by his permission, are always more precious than those which are the offspring of our own will; for it is a general rule, that wherever there is less of our own choice, God is better pleased, and we ourselves derive greater profit."[28] St. Teresa taught the same thing: "We gain more in one day by the oppositions which come to us from God or our neighbor than by ten years of mortifications of self-infliction."[29] Wherefore St. Mary Magdalene of Pazzi made the generous declaration, that there could not be found in the whole world an affliction so severe, but what she would gladly bear with the thought that it came from God; and, in fact, during the five years of severe trial which the saint underwent, it was enough to restore peace to her soul to remember that it was by the will of God that she so suffered. Ah, God, that infinite treasure is cheaply purchased at any cost! Father Hippolytus Durazzo used to say, "Purchase God at what cost you will, he can never be dear."

Let us then beseech God to make us worthy of his love; for if we did but once perfectly love him, all the goods of this earth would seem to us but as smoke and dirt, and we should relish ignominies and afflictions as delights. Let us hear what St. John Chrysostom says of a soul wholly given up to Almighty God: "He who has attained the perfect love of God seems to be alone on the earth, he no longer cares either for glory or ignominy, he scorns temptations and afflictions, he loses all relish and appetite for created things. And as nothing in this world brings him any support or repose, he goes incessantly in search of his beloved without ever feeling wearied; so that when he toils, when he eats, when he is watching, or when sleeping, in every action and word, all his thoughts and desires are fixed upon finding his beloved; because his heart is where his treasure is."[note]

Affections and Prayers.

My dear and beloved Jesus, my treasure, I have deserved by my offences never more to be allowed to love Thee; but by Thy merits, I entreat Thee, make me worthy of Thy pure love. I love Thee above all things; and I repent with my whole heart, of having ever despised Thee, and driven Thee from my soul; but now I love Thee more than myself; I love Thee with all my heart, O infinite good! I love Thee, I love Thee, I love Thee, and I have not a wish besides that of loving Thee perfectly; nor have I a fear besides that of ever seeing myself deprived of Thy love. O my most loving Redeemer, enable me to know how great a good Thou art, and how great is the love Thou hast borne me in order to oblige me to love Thee! Ah, my God, suffer me not to live any longer unmindful of so much goodness! Enough have I offended Thee, I will never leave Thee again; I wish to employ all the remainder of my days in loving Thee, and in pleasing Thee. My Jesus, my Love, lend me Thine aid; help a sinner who wishes to love Thee and to be wholly Thine own.

O Mary my hope, thy Son hears thee; pray to him in my behalf and obtain for me the grace of loving him perfectly!

In this chapter we have spoken of patience in general; in Chapter X. we shall treat more particularly of occasions in which we have especially to practice patience.

2

— · —

CHARITY IS KIND

HE THAT LOVES JESUS CHRIST LOVES MEEKNESS

The spirit of meekness is peculiar to God: My spirit is sweet above honey.[1] Hence it is that a soul that loves God also loves all those whom God loves, namely, her neighbors; so that she eagerly seeks every occasion of helping all, of consoling all, and of making all happy as far as she can. St. Francis de Sales, who was the master and model of holy meekness, says, "Humble meekness is the virtue of virtues, which God has so much recommended to us; therefore we should endeavor to practice it always and in all things."[2] Hence the saint gives us this rule: "What you see can be done with love, do it; and what you see cannot be done without offence, leave it undone."[3] He means, when it can be omitted without offending God; because an offence of God must always, and as quickly as possible, be prevented by him who is bound to prevent it.

This meekness should be particularly observed towards the poor, who, by reason of their poverty, are often harshly treated by men. It should likewise be especially practiced towards the sick who are suffering under infirmities, and for the most part meet with small help from others. Meekness is more especially to be observed in our behavior towards enemies: Overcome evil with good.[4] Hatred must be overcome by love, and persecution by meekness; thus, the saints acted, and so they conciliated the affections of their most exasperated enemies.

"There is nothing," says St. Francis de Sales, "that gives so much edification to our neighbor as meekness of behavior."[5] The saint, therefore, was generally seen smiling, and with a countenance beaming with charity, which gave a tone to all his words and actions. This gave occasion to St. Vincent of Paul [6] to declare that he never knew a kinder man in his life. He said further that it seemed to him that in his lordship of Sales was a true likeness of Jesus Christ. Even in refusing what he could not in conscience comply with, he did so with such sweetness, that all, though unsuccessful in their requests, went away satisfied and well-disposed towards him. He was gentle towards all, towards Superiors, towards equals and inferiors, at home and abroad; in contrast with some, who, as the saint used to say, "seemed angels abroad, but were devils at home."[7] Moreover, the saint, in his conduct towards servants, never complained of their remissness; at most he would give them an admonition, but always in the gentlest terms. And this is a thing most praiseworthy in Superiors.

The Superior should use all kindness towards those under him. When telling them what they have to do, he should rather request than command. St. Vincent of Paul said: "A Superior will never find a better means of being readily obeyed than meekness." And to the same effect was the saying of St. Jane Frances of Chantal: "I have tried various methods of governing, but I have not found any better than that of meekness and forbearance."[8]

And more than this, the Superior should be kind even in the correction of faults. It is one thing to correct with firmness, and another with harshness; it is needful at times to correct with firmness, when the fault is serious, and especially if it be repeated after the subject has already been admonished of it; but let us always be on our guard against harsh and angry correction; he that corrects with anger does more harm than good. This is that bitter zeal reproved by St. James. Some make a boast of keeping their family in order by severity, and they say it is the only successful method of treatment; but St. James speaks not so: But if you have bitter zeal ... glory not.[9] If on some rare occasion it be necessary to speak a cross word, in order to bring the offender to a proper sense of his fault, yet in the end we ought invariably to leave him with a gentle countenance and a word of kindness. Wounds must be healed after the fashion of the good Samaritan in the Gospel, with wine and oil: "But as oil," said St. Francis de Sales, "always swims on the surface of all other liquors, so must meekness prevail over all our actions." And when it occurs that the person under correction is agitated, then the reprehension must be deferred till his anger has subsided, or else we should only increase his indignation. The Canon Regular St. John said: "When the house is on fire, one must not cast wood into the flames."

You know not of what spirit you are.[10] Such were the words of Jesus Christ to his disciples James and John, when they would have brought down chastisements on the Samaritans for expelling them from their country. Ah, said the Lord to them, and what spirit is this? this is not my spirit, which is sweet and gentle; for I am come not to destroy but to save souls: The Son of Man came not to destroy souls, but to save.[11] And would you induce me to destroy them? Oh, hush! and never make the like request to me, for such is not according to my spirit. And, in fact, with what meekness did Jesus Christ treat the adulteress! Woman, said He, hath no man condemned thee? Neither will I condemn thee! Go, and now sin no more.[12] He was satisfied with merely warning her not to sin again and sent her away in peace. With what meekness, again, did he seek the conversion of the Samaritan woman, and so, in fact, converted her! He first asked her to give him something to drink; then he said to her: If thou didst know who He is that saith to thee, give me to drink! and then he revealed to her that he was the expected Messiah. And, again, with what meekness did he strive to convert the impious Judas, admitting him to eat of the same dish with him, washing his feet and admonishing him in the very act of his betrayal: Judas, and dost thou thus betray me with a kiss? Judas, dost thou betray the Son of Man with a kiss?[13] And see how he converted Peter after his denial of him! And the Lord turning, looked on Peter.[14] On leaving the house of the high priest, without making him a single reproach, he cast on him a look of tenderness, and thus converted him; and so effectually did he convert him, that during his whole lifelong Peter never ceased to bewail the injury he had done to his Master.

Oh, how much more is to be gained by meekness than by harshness! St. Francis de Sales said there was nothing more bitter than the bitter almond, but if made into a preserve, it becomes sweet and agreeable: thus corrections, though in their nature very unpleasant, are rendered pleasant by love and meekness, and so are attended with more beneficial results. St. Vincent of Paul said of himself, that in the government of his own congregation he had never corrected any one with severity, except on three occasions, when he supposed there was reason to do so, but that he regretted it ever afterwards, because he found it turned out badly; whereas he had always admirably succeeded by gentle correction.[15]

St. Francis de Sales obtained from others whatever he wished by his meek behavior; and by this means he managed to gain the most hardened sinners to God. It was the same with St. Vincent of Paul, who taught his disciples this maxim: "Affability, love, and humility have a wonderful efficacy in winning the hearts of men, and in prevailing on them to undertake things most repugnant to nature." He once gave a great sinner to the care of one of his Fathers, to bring him to sentiments of true repentance; but that Father, despite all his endeavors, found his labor fruitless, so that he begged the saint to speak a word to him. The saint accordingly spoke with him and converted him. That sinner subsequently declared that the singular sweetness of Father Vincent had worked upon his heart. Wherefore it was that the saint could not bear his missionaries to treat sinners with severity; and he told them that the infernal spirit took advantage of the strictness of some to work the greater ruin of souls.

Kindness should be always observed towards all on all occasions and. St. Bernard remarks,[16] that certain persons are gentle as long as things fall out to their taste; but scarcely do they experience some opposition or contradiction than they are instantly on fire, like Mount Vesuvius itself. Such as these may be called burning coals but hidden under embers. Whoever would become a saint, must, during this life, resemble the lily among thorns, which, however much it may be pricked by them, never ceases to be a lily; that is, it is always equally sweet and serene. The soul that loves God maintains an imperturbable peace of heart; and she shows this in her very countenance, being ever mistress of herself, alike in prosperity and adversity, according to the lines of Cardinal Petrucci:

"Of outward things he views the varying guise,
While in his soul's most inmost depth
Undimmed God's image lies."

Adversity brings out a person's real character. St. Francis de Sales very tenderly loved the Order of the Visitation, which had cost him so much labor. He saw it several times in imminent danger of dissolution on account of the persecutions it underwent; but the saint never for a moment lost his peace, and was ready, if such was the will of God, to see it entirely destroyed; and then it was that he said: "For some time back the trying oppositions and secret contrarieties which have befallen me afford me so sweet a peace, that nothing can equal it; and they give me such an earnest of the immediate union of my soul with God, that, in truth, they form the sole desire of my heart."[17]

Whenever it happens that we must reply to someone who insults us, let us be careful to answer with meekness: A mild answer breaketh wrath.[18] A mild reply is enough to quench every spark of anger. And in case we feel irritated, it is best to keep silent, because then it seems only just to give vent to all that rises to our lips; but when our passion has subsided, we shall see that all our words were full of faults.

And when it happens that we ourselves commit some fault, we must also practice meekness in our own regard. To be exasperated at ourselves after a fault is not humility, but a subtle pride, as if we were anything else than the weak and miserable things that we are. St. Teresa said: "The humility that disturbs does not come from God, but from the devil."[19] To be angry at ourselves after the commission of a fault is a fault worse than the one committed, and will be the occasion of many other faults; it will make us leave off our devotions, prayers, and communions; or if we do practice them, they will be done very badly. St. Aloysius Gonzaga said that we cannot see in troubled waters, and that the devil fishes in them. A soul that is troubled knows little of God and of what it ought to do. Whenever, therefore, we fall into any fault, we should turn to God with humility and confidence, and craving his forgiveness, say to him, with St. Catharine of Genoa: "O Lord, this is the produce of my own garden! I love Thee with my whole heart, and I repent of the displeasure I have given Thee! I will never do the like again: grant me Thy assistance!"

Affections and Prayers.

O blessed chains that bind the soul with God, oh, enfold me still closer, and in links so firm that I may never be able to loosen myself from the love of my God! My Jesus, I love Thee; O treasure, O life of my soul, to Thee I cling, and I give myself wholly unto Thee! No, indeed, my beloved Lord, I wish never more to cease to love Thee. Thou who, to atone for my sins, didst allow Thyself to be bound as a criminal, and so bound to be led to death through the streets of Jerusalem,—Thou who didst consent to be nailed to the cross, and didst not leave it until life itself had left Thee, oh, suffer me never to be separated from Thee again; I regret above every other evil, to have at one time turned my back upon Thee, and henceforth I purpose by Thy grace to die rather than to give Thee the slightest displeasure. O my Jesus, I abandon myself to Thee. I love Thee with my whole heart; I love Thee more than myself. I have offended Thee in times past; but now I bitterly repent of it, and I would willingly die of grief. Oh, draw me entirely to Thyself! I renounce all sensible consolations; I wish for Thee alone, and nothing more. Make me love Thee, and then do with me what Thou wilt. O Mary, my hope, bind me to Jesus; and grant me to live and die in union with him, to come one day to the happy kingdom, where I shall have no more fear of ever being separated from his love!

— • —

Charity Envieth Not

The Soul that Loves Jesus Christ Does Not Envy the Great Ones of this World, but Only Those Who are Greater Lovers of Jesus Christ

St. Gregory explains this next characteristic of charity in saying, that as charity despises all earthly greatness, it cannot possibly provoke her envy. "She envieth not, because, as she desireth nothing in this world, she cannot envy earthly prosperity."[1]

Hence, we must distinguish two kinds of envy, one evil and the other holy. The evil kind is that which envies and repines at the worldly goods possessed by others on this earth. But holy envy, so far from wishing to be like, rather compassionate the great ones of the world, who live in the midst of honors and earthly pleasures. She seeks and desires God alone and has no other aim besides that of loving him as much as she can; and therefore, she has a pious envy of those who love him more than she does, for she would, if possible, surpass the very seraphim in loving him.

This is the sole end which pious souls have in view on earth—an end which so charms and ravishes the heart of God with love, that it causes him to say: Thou hast wounded My heart, My sister; My spouse, thou hast wounded My heart with one of thy eyes.[2] By "one of thy eyes" is meant that one end which the espoused soul has in all her devotions and thoughts, namely, to please Almighty God. Men of the world look on things with many eyes, that is, have several inordinate views in their actions; as, for instance, to please others, to become honored, to obtain riches, and if nothing else, at least to please themselves; but the saints have but a single eye, with which they keep in view, in all that they do, the sole pleasure of God; and with David they say: What have I in heaven, and besides Thee what do I desire upon earth?[3] What do I wish, O my God, in this world or in the next, save Thee alone? Thou art my riches, Thou art the only Lord of my heart. "Let the rich," said St. Paulinus, "enjoy their riches, let the kings enjoy their kingdoms, Thou, O Christ, art my treasure and my kingdom!"[4]

And here we must remark that we must not only perform good works, but we must perform them well. In order that our works may be good and perfect, they must be done with the sole end of pleasing God. This was the admirable praise bestowed on Jesus Christ: He hath done all things well.[5] Many actions may in themselves be praiseworthy, but from being performed for some other purpose than for the glory of God, they are often of little or no value in his sight. St. Mary Magdalene of Pazzi said, "God rewards our actions by the weight of pure intention."[6] As much as to say, that according as our intention is pure, so does the Lord accept of and reward our actions. But, O God, how difficult it is to find an action done solely for Thee! I remember a holy old man, a religious, who had labored much in the service of God, and died in the reputation of sanctity; now one day, as he cast a glance back at his past life, he said to me in a tone of sadness and fear, "Wo is me! when I consider all the actions of my past life, I do not find one done entirely for God." Oh, this accursed self-love, that makes us lose all or the greater part of the fruit of our good actions! How many in their most holy employments, as of preaching, hearing confessions, giving missions, labor and exert themselves very much, and gain little or nothing because they do not regard God alone, but worldly honor, or self-interest, or the vanity of making an appearance, or at least their own inclination!

Our Lord has said, Take heed that yon do not your justice before men, to be seen by them; otherwise you shall not have a reward of your Father who is in heaven.[7] He that works for his own gratification already receives his wages: Amen I say to you, they have received their reward.[8] But a reward, indeed, which dwindles into a little smoke, or the pleasure of a day that quickly vanishes, and confers no benefit on the soul. The Prophet Aggeus says, that whoever labors for anything else than to please God, puts his reward in a sack full of holes, which, when he comes to open, he finds entirely empty: And he that hath earned wages, put them into a bag with holes.[9] And hence it is that such persons, in the event of their not gaining the object for which they entered on some undertaking, are thrown into great trouble. This is a sign that they had not in view the glory of God alone. He that undertakes a thing solely for the glory of God, is not troubled at all, though his undertaking may fail of success; for, in truth, by working with a pure intention, he has already gained his object, which was to please Almighty God.

The following are the signs which indicate whether we work solely for God in any spiritual undertaking. 1. If we are not disturbed at the failure of our plans, because when we see it is not God's will, neither is it any longer our will. 2. If we rejoice at the good done by others, as heartily as if we ourselves had done it. 3. If we have no preference for one charge more than for another, but willingly accept that which obedience to Superiors enjoins us. 4. If after our actions we do not seek the thanks or approbation of others, nor are in any way affected if we be found fault with or scolded, being satisfied with having pleased God. And if when the world applauds us we are not puffed up, but meet the vain glory, which might make, itself felt, with the reply of the venerable John of Avila: "Get away, thou comest too late, for all has been already given to God."

This is to enter into the joy of the Lord; that is, to enjoy the enjoyment of God, as is promised to his faithful servants: Well done, thou good and faithful servant; because thou hast been faithful over a few things, ... enter thou into the joy of thy Lord.[10] And if it falls to our lot to do something pleasing to God, what more, asks St. John Chrysostom, can we desire? "If thou art found worthy to perform something that pleases God, dost thou seek other recompense than this?"[11] The greatest reward, the brightest fortune, that can befall a creature, is to give pleasure to his Creator.

And this is what Jesus Christ looks for from a soul that loves him: Put me, he says, as a seal upon thy heart, as a seal upon thy arm.[12] He desires us to place him as a seal on our heart and on our arm: on our heart, in order that whatever we intend doing, we may intend solely for the love of God; on our arm, in order that whatever we do, all may be done to please God; so that God may be always the sole end of all our thoughts and of all our actions. St. Teresa said, that he who would become a saint must live free from every other desire than that of pleasing God; and her first daughter, the Venerable Beatrice of the Incarnation, said, "No sum whatever could repay the slightest thing done for God."[13] And with reason; for all things done to please God are acts of charity which unite us to God, and obtain for us ever lasting rewards.

Purity of intention is called the heavenly alchemy by which iron is turned into gold; that is to say, the most trivial actions (such as to work, to take one's meals, to take recreation or repose), when done for God, become the gold of holy love. Wherefore St.

Mary Magdalene of Pazzi believes for certain that those who do all with a pure intention, go straight to Paradise, without passing through purgatory. It is related (in the Spiritual Treasury) that it was the custom of a pious hermit, before setting about any work, to pause a little, and lift his eyes to heaven; on being questioned why he did so, he replied, "I am taking my aim." By which he meant, that as the archer, before shooting his arrow, takes his aim, that he may not miss the mark, so before each action he made God his aim, in order that it might be sure of pleasing him. We should do the same; and even during the performance of our actions, it is very good for us from time to time to renew our good intention.

Those who have nothing else in view in their undertakings than the divine will, enjoy that holy liberty of spirit which belongs to the children of God; and this enables them to embrace everything that pleases Jesus Christ, however revolting it may be to their own self-love or human respect. The love of Jesus Christ establishes his lovers in a state of total indifference; so that all is the same to them, be it sweet or bitter; they desire nothing for their own pleasure, but all for the pleasure of God. With the same feelings of peace, they address themselves to small and great works; to the pleasant and the unpleasant: it is enough for them if they please God.

Many, on the other hand, are willing to serve God, but it must be in such an employment, in such a place, with such companions, or under such circumstances, or else they either quit the work, or do it with an ill-will. Such persons have not freedom of spirit but are slaves of self-love; and on that account gain very little merit by what they do; they lead a troubled life, because the yoke of Jesus Christ becomes a burden to them. The true lovers of Jesus Christ care only to do what pleases him; and for the reason that it pleases him, when he wills, and where he wills, and in the manner he wills: and whether he wishes to employ them in a state of life honored by the world, or in a life of obscurity and insignificance. This is what is meant by loving Jesus Christ with a pure love; and in this we ought to exercise ourselves, battling against the craving of our self-love, which would urge us to seek important and honorable functions, and such as suit our inclinations.

We must, moreover, be detached from all exercises, even spiritual ones, when the Lord wishes us to be occupied in other works of his good pleasure. One day, Father Alvarez, finding himself overwhelmed with business, was anxious to get rid of it, in order to go and pray, because it seemed to him that during that time he was not with God; but our Lord then said to him: "Though I do not keep thee with me, let it suffice thee that I make use of thee."[14] This is a profitable lesson for those who are sometimes disturbed at being obliged, by obedience or by charity, to leave their accustomed devotions; let them be assured that such disturbances on like occasions do not come from God, but either from the devil or from self-love. "Give pleasure to God and die." This is the grand maxim of the saints.

Affections and Prayers.

O my Eternal God, I offer Thee my whole heart; but what sort of heart, O God, is it that I offer Thee? A heart, created, indeed, to love Thee; but which, instead of loving Thee, has so many times rebelled against Thee. But behold, my Jesus, if there was a time when my heart rebelled against Thee, now it is deeply grieved and penitent for the displeasure it has given Thee. Yes, my dear Redeemer, I am sorry for having despised Thee; and I am determined to do all to obey Thee, and to love Thee at every cost. Oh, draw me wholly to Thy love; do this for the sake of the love which made Thee die for me on the cross. I love Thee, my Jesus; I love Thee with all my soul; I love Thee more than myself, O true and only lover of my soul; for I find none but Thee who have sacrificed their life for me. I weep to think that I have been so ungrateful to Thee. Unhappy that I am! I was already lost; but I trust that by Thy grace Thou hast restored me to life. And this shall he my life, to love Thee always, my sovereign good. Make me love Thee, O infinite love, and I ask Thee for nothing more!

O Mary my mother, accept of me for thy servant, and gain acceptance for me with Jesus thy Son.

CHARITY DEALETH NOT PERVERSLY

HE THAT LOVES JESUS CHRIST AVOIDS LUKEWARMNESS AND SEEKS PERFECTION; THE MEANS OF WHICH ARE: 1. DESIRE; 2. RESOLUTION; 3. MENTAL PRAYER; 4. COMMUNION; 5. PRAYER.

St. Gregory, in his explanation of these words, "dealeth not perversely," says that charity, giving herself up more and more to the love of God, ignores whatever is not right and holy.[1] The Apostle had already written to the same effect, when he calls charity a bond that unites the most perfect virtues together in the soul. Have charity, which is the bond of perfection.[2] And whereas charity delights in perfection, she consequently abhors that lukewarmness with which some persons serve God, to the great risk of losing charity, divine grace, their very soul, and their all.

I.

Lukewarmness.

It must be observed that there are two kinds of tepidity or lukewarmness: the one unavoidable, the other avoidable.

I.—From the lukewarmness that is unavoidable, the saints themselves are not exempt; and this comprises all the failings that are committed by us without full con sent, but merely from our natural frailty. Such are, for example, distractions at prayers, interior disquietudes, useless words, vain curiosity, the wish to appear, tastes in eating and drinking, the movements of concupiscence not instantly repressed, and such like. We ought to avoid these defects as much as we possibly can; but, owing to the weakness of our nature, caused by the infection of sin, it is impossible to avoid them altogether. We ought, indeed, to detest them after committing them, because they are displeasing to God; but, as we remarked in the preceding chapter, we ought to beware of making them a subject of alarm or disquietude. St. Francis de Sales writes as follows: "All such thoughts as create disquietude are not from God, who is the prince of peace; but they proceed always from the devil, or from self-love, or from the good opinion which we have of ourselves."[3] Such thoughts, therefore, as disturb us, must be straightway rejected, and made no account of.

It was also said by the same saint, with regard to indeliberate faults, that as they were involuntarily committed, so are they cancelled involuntarily. An act of sorrow, an act of love, is sufficient to cancel them. The Venerable Sister Mary Crucified, a Benedictine nun, saw once a globe of fire, on which several straws were cast, and were all forthwith reduced to ashes. She was given to understand by this figure that one act of divine love, made with fervor, destroys all the defects that we may have in our soul. The same effect is produced by the holy Communion; according to what we find in the Council of Trent, where the Eucharist is called "an antidote by which we are freed from daily faults."[4] Thus the like faults, though they are indeed faults, do not hinder perfection that is, our advancing toward perfection; because in the present life no one attains perfection before he arrives at the kingdom of the blessed.

II. The tepidity, then, that does hinder perfection is that tepidity which is avoidable when a person commits deliberate venial faults; because all these faults committed with open eyes can effectually be avoided by the divine grace, even in the present life. Wherefore St. Teresa said: "May God deliver you from deliberate sin, however small it may be."[5] Such, for example, are willful untruths, little detractions, imprecations, expressions of anger, derisions of one's neighbor, cutting words, speeches of self-esteem, animosities nourished in the heart, inordinate attachments to persons of a different sex. "These are a sort of worm" (wrote the same saint) "which is not detected before it has eaten into the virtues."[6] Hence, in another place, the saint gave this admonition: "By means of small things the devil goes about making holes for great things to enter."[7]

We should therefore tremble at such deliberate faults; since they cause God to close his hands from bestowing upon us his clearer lights and stronger helps, and they deprive us of spiritual sweetness; and the result of them is to make the soul perform all spiritual exercises with great weariness and pain; and so, in course of time, she begins to leave off prayer, Communions, visits to the Blessed Sacrament, and novenas; and, in fine, she will probably leave off all, as has not unfrequently been the case with many unhappy souls.

This is the meaning of that threat which our Lord makes to the tepid: Thou art neither cold nor hot; I would thou wert cold or hot: but because thou art lukewarm ... I will begin to vomit thee out of My mouth.[8] How wonderful! He says, I would thou wert cold! What! and is it better to be cold, that is, deprived of grace, than to be tepid? Yes, in a certain sense it is better to be cold; because a person who is cold may more easily change his life, being stung by the reproaches of conscience; whereas a tepid person contracts the habit of slumbering on in his faults, without bestowing a thought, or taking any trouble to correct himself; and thus he makes his cure, as it were, desperate. St. Gregory says, "Tepidity, which has cooled down from fervor, is a hopeless state."[9] The Ven. Father Louis da Ponte said that he had committed many defects during his life; but that he never had made a truce with his faults. Some there are who shake hands with their faults, and from that springs their ruin; especially when the fault is accompanied with some passionate attachment of self-esteem, of ambition, of liking to be seen, of heaping up money, of resentment against a neighbor, or of inordinate affection for a per son of different sex. In such cases there is great danger of those hairs, as it were, becoming chains, as St. Francis of Assisi said, which will drag down the soul to hell. At all events, such a soul will never become a saint, and will forfeit that beautiful crown, which God had prepared for her, had she faithfully corresponded to grace. The bird no sooner feels itself loosed from the snare than it immediately flies; the soul, as soon as she is loosed from earthly attachments, immediately flies to God; but while she is bound, though it be but by the slightest thread, it is enough to prevent her from flying to God. Oh, how many spiritual people there are who do not become saints, because they will not do themselves the violence to break away from certain little attachments!

All the evil arises from the little love they have for Jesus Christ. Those who are puffed up with self-esteem; those who frequently take to heart occurrences that fall out contrary to their wishes; who practice great indulgence towards themselves on account of their health; who keep their heart open to external objects, and the mind always distracted, with an eagerness to listen to, and to know, so many things that have nothing to do with the service of God, but merely serve to gratify private curiosity; who are ready to resent every little inattention from others, and consequently are often troubled, and grow remiss in prayer and recollection. One moment they are all devotion and joy, the next all impatience and melancholy, just as things happen, according to or against their humor; all such persons do not love Jesus Christ, or love him very little, and cast discredit on true devotion.

But suppose anyone should find himself sunk in this unhappy state of tepidity, what has he to do? Certainly, it is a hard thing for a soul grown lukewarm to resume her ancient fervor; but our Lord has said, that what man cannot do, God can very well do. The things that are impossible with man, are possible with God.[10] Whoever prays and employs the means is sure to accomplish his desire.

II.

Remedies against Lukewarmness.

The means to cast off tepidity, and to tread in the path of perfection, are five in number: 1. The desire for perfection; 2. The resolution to attain it; 3. Mental prayer; 4. Frequent Holy Communion; 5. Prayer.

1. Desire of Perfection.

The first means, then, is the desire of perfection. Pious desires are the wings which lift us up from earth; for, as St. Laurence Justinian says, desire "supplies strength, and renders pain lighter:"[11] on the one hand it gives strength to walk towards perfection, and on the other hand it lightens the fatigue of the journey. He who has a real desire of perfection fails not to advance continually towards it; and so advancing, he must finally arrive at it. On the contrary, he who has not the desire of perfection will always go backwards, and always find himself more imperfect than before. St. Augustine says, that "not to go forward in the way of God is to go backward."[12] He that makes no efforts to advance will find himself carried backward by the current of his corrupt nature.

They, then, who say "God does not wish us all to be saints" make a great mistake. Yes, for St. Paul says, This is the Will of God, your sanctification.[13] God wishes all to be saints, and each one according to his state of life: the religious as a religious; the secular as a secular; the priest as a priest; the married as married; the man of business as a man of business; the soldier as a soldier; and so of every other state of life.

Most beautiful, indeed, are the instructions which my great patroness St. Teresa gives on this subject. She says, in one place, "Let us enlarge our thoughts; for hence we shall derive immense good." Elsewhere she says: "We must beware of having poor desires; but rather put our confidence in God, in order that, by forcing ourselves continually onwards, we may by degrees arrive where, by the divine grace, so many saints have arrived."[14] And in confirmation of this she quoted her own experience, having known how courageous souls make considerable progress in a short period of time. "Because," said she, "the Lord takes as much delight in our desires, as if they were put into execution." In another place she says: "Almighty God does not confer extraordinary favors, except where his love has been earnestly sought after."[15] Again, in another passage, she remarks: "God does not fail to repay every good desire even in this life,[16] for he is the friend of generous souls, provided only they do not trust in themselves."[17] This saint herself was endowed with just such a spirit of generosity; so that she once even said to our Lord, that were she to behold others in paradise enjoying him more than herself, she should not care; but were she to behold any one loving him more than she should love him, this she declared she knew not how she could endure.[18]

We must, therefore, have a great courage: The Lord is good to the soul that seek him.[19] God is surpassingly good and liberal towards a soul that heartily seeks him. Neither can past sins prove a hindrance to our becoming saints if we only have the sincere desire to become so. St. Teresa remarks: "The devil strives to make us think it pride to entertain lofty desires, and to wish to imitate the saints; but it is of great service to encourage ourselves with the desire of great things, because, although the soul has not all at once the necessary strength, yet she nevertheless makes a bold fight, and rapidly advances."[20]

The Apostle writes: To them that love God, all things work together unto good.[21] And the gloss or ancient commentary adds "even sins;"[22] even past sins can contribute to our sanctification, inasmuch as the recollection of them keeps us more humble, and more grateful, when we witness the favors which God lavishes upon us, after all our outrages against him. I am capable of nothing (the sinner should say), nor do I deserve anything; I deserve nothing but hell; but I must deal with a God of infinite bounty, who has promised to listen to all that pray to him. Now, as he has rescued me from a state of damnation, and wishes me to become holy, and now proffers me his help, I can certainly become a saint, not by my own strength, but by the grace of my God, who strengthens me: I can do all things in Him that strengthens me.[23] When, therefore, we have once good desires, we must take courage, and trusting in God, endeavor to put them in execution; but if afterwards we encounter any obstacle in our spiritual enterprises, let us repose quietly on the will of God. God's will must be preferred before every good desire of our own. St. Mary Magdalene of Pazzi would sooner have remained void of all perfection than possess it without the will of God.

2. Resolution.

The second means of perfection is the resolution to belong wholly to God. Many are called to perfection; they are urged on towards it by grace, they conceive a desire of it; but because they never really resolve to acquire it, they live and die in the ill-odor their tepid and imperfect life. The desire for perfection is not enough if it is not followed up by a stern resolve to attain it. How many souls feed themselves on desires alone, but never make withal one step in the way of God! It is of such desires that the wise man speaks when he says: Desires kill the slothful.[24] The slothful man is ever desiring, but never resolves to take the means suitable to his state of life to become a saint. He says: "Oh, if I were but in solitude, and not in this house! Oh, if I could but go and reside in another monastery, I would give myself entirely up to God!" And meanwhile he cannot support a certain companion; he cannot put up with a word of contradiction; he is dissipated about many useless cares; he commits a thousand faults of gluttony of curiosity, and of pride; and yet he sighs out to the wind: "Oh, if I had but!" or "Oh, if I could but!" etc. Such desires do more harm than good; because some regale themselves upon them, and in the meantime go on leading a life of imperfection. It was a saying of St. Francis de Sales: "I do not approve of a person who, being engaged in some duty or vocation, stops to sigh for some other kind of life than is compatible with his actual position, or for other exercises unfitted for his present state; for it merely serves to dissipate his heart, and makes him languish in his necessary duties."[25]

We must, therefore, desire perfection, and resolutely take the means towards it. St. Teresa says: "God only looks for one resolution on our part and will afterwards do all the rest himself:[26] the devil has no fear of irresolute souls."[27] For this reason mental prayer must be used, in order to take the means which, lead to perfection. Some make much prayer, but never come to a practical conclusion. The same saint said: "I would rather have a short prayer, which produces great fruits, than a prayer of many years, wherein a soul never gets further than resolving to do something worthy of Almighty God."[28] And elsewhere she says: "I have learned by experience that whoever, at the beginning, brings himself to the resolution of doing some great work, however difficult it may be, if he does so to please God, he has no reason to be afraid."

The first resolution must be to make every effort, and to die rather than commit any deliberate sin whatever, however small it may be. It is true that all our endeavors, without the divine assistance, cannot enable us to vanquish temptations; but God wishes us on our part frequently to use this violence with ourselves, because then he will afterwards supply us with his grace, will succor our weakness, and enable us to gain the victory. This resolution removes from us every obstacle to our going forward, and at the same time gives us great courage, because it affords us an assurance of being in the grace of God. St. Francis de Sales writes: "The best security we can possess in this world of being in the grace of God, consists not indeed in feeling that we have his love, but in a pure and irrevocable abandonment of our entire being into his hands, and in the firm resolution of never consenting to any sin, either great or small."[29] This is what is meant by being of a delicate conscience. Be it observed that it is one thing to be of a delicate conscience, and another to be of a scrupulous conscience. To be of a delicate conscience is requisite to become a saint; but to be scrupulous is a defect and does harm; and on this account we must obey our directors, and rise above scruples, which are nothing else but vain and unreasonable alarms.

Hence it is necessary to resolve on choosing the best, not only what is agreeable to God, but what is most agreeable to him, without any reserve. St. Francis de Sales says: "We must start with a strong and constant resolution to give ourselves wholly to God, and protest to him that for the future we wish to be his without any Deserve, and then we must afterwards often renew this same resolution."[30] St. Andrew Avellini made a vow to advance daily in perfection. It is not necessary for everyone who wishes to become a saint to make it a matter of a vow; but he must endeavor every day to make some steps forward in perfection. St. Laurence Justinian has written: "When a person is really making way, he feels in himself a continual desire of advancing; and the more he improves in perfection, the more this desire increases; because as his interior light increases each day more and more, he seems to himself always to be wanting in every virtue, and to be doing no good at all; and if, perchance, he is aware of some good he does, it always appears to him very imperfect, and he makes small account of it. The consequence is, he is continually laboring to acquire perfection without ever feeling wearied."

And we must begin quickly, and not wait for the morrow. Who knows whether we shall afterwards find time or not! Ecclesiastes counsels us: Whatsoever thy hand is able to do, do it earnestly.[31] What thou canst do, do it quickly, and defer it not; and he adduces the reason why: For neither work, nor reason, nor wisdom, nor knowledge shall be in hell, whither thou art hastening.[32] Because in the next life there is no more time to work, nor free will to merit, nor prudence to do well, nor wisdom or experience to take good counsel by, for after death what is done is done.

A nun of the convent of Torre de Specchi in Rome, whose name was Sister Bonaventura, led a very lukewarm sort of life. There came a religious, Father Lancicius, to give the spiritual exercises to the nuns, and Sister Bonaventura, feeling no inclination to shake off her tepidity, began to listen to the exercises with no good will. But at the very first sermon she was won by divine grace, so that she immediately went to the feet of the Father who preached, and said to him, with a tone of real determination, "Father, I wish to become a saint, and quickly a saint." And, by the assistance of God, she did so; for she lived only eight months after that event, and during that short time she lived and died a saint.

David said: And I said, now have I begun.[33] So likewise exclaimed St. Charles Borromeo: "To-day I begin to serve God." And we should act in the same way as if we had hitherto done no good whatever; for, indeed, all that we do for God is nothing, since we are bound to do it. Let us therefore each day resolve to begin afresh to belong wholly to God. Neither let us stop to observe what or how others do. They who become truly saints are few. St. Bernard says: "One cannot be perfect without being singular."[34] If we would imitate the common run of men, we should always remain imperfect, as for the most part they are. We must overcome all, renounce all, to gain all. St. Teresa said: "Because we do not come to the conclusion of giving all our affection to God, so neither does he give all his love to us."[35] Oh, God, how little is all that is given to Jesus Christ, who has given his blood and his life for us! "However much we give," says the same saint, "is but dirt, in comparison of one single drop of blood shed for us by our Blessed Lord."[36] The saints know not how to spare themselves, when there is a question of pleasing a God who gave himself wholly, without reserve, on purpose to oblige us to deny him nothing. St. John Chrysostom wrote: "He gave all to thee and kept nothing for himself."[37] God has bestowed his entire self upon thee; there is, then, no excuse for thee to behave reservedly with God. He has even died for us all, says the Apostle, in order that each one of us may live only for him who died for us: Christ died for all; that they also who live may not now live to themselves, but unto Him who died for them.[38]

3. Mental Prayer.

The third means of becoming a saint is mental prayer. John Gerson writes:[39] "That he who does not meditate on the eternal truths cannot, without a miracle, lead the life of a Christian. The reason is, because without mental prayer light fails us, and we walk in the dark. The truths of faith are not seen by the eyes of the body, but by the eyes of the mind, when we meditate; he that fails to meditate on them, fails to see them, and therefore walks in the dark; and being in the dark, he easily grows attached to sensible things, for the sake of which he then comes to despise the eternal." St. Teresa wrote as follows to the Bishop of Osma: "Although we seem to discover in ourselves no imperfections; yet, when God opens the eyes of the soul, which he is wont to do in prayer, then they plainly appear."[40] And St. Bernard had before said, that he who does not meditate "does not abhor himself, merely because he does not know himself."[41] "Prayer," says the saint, "regulates the affections, directs the actions,"[42] keeps the affections of the soul in order, and directs all our actions to God; but without prayer the affections become attached to the earth, the actions conform themselves to the affections, and in this manner all runs into disorder.

We read of an awful example of this in the life of the Venerable Sister Mary Crucified of Sicily. Whilst this servant of God was praying, she heard a devil making a boast that he had succeeded in withdrawing a religious from the community-prayer; and she saw in spirit, that after this omission the devil tempted her to consent to a grievous sin, and that she was on the point of yielding. She forthwith accosted her, and by a timely admonition prevented her from falling. Abbé Dioclès said, that whoever leaves off prayer "very shortly becomes either a beast or a devil."[43]

He therefore that leaves off prayer will leave off loving Jesus Christ. Prayer is the blessed furnace in which the fire of holy love is enkindled and kept alive: And in my meditation a fire shall flame out.[44] It was said by St. Catharine of Bologna: "The person that foregoes the practice of prayer cuts that string which binds the soul to God." It follows that the devil, finding the soul cold in divine love, will have little difficulty in inducing her to partake of some poisonous fruit or other. St. Teresa said, on the contrary, "Whosoever perseveres in prayer, let him hold for a certainty, that with however many sins the devil may surround him, the Lord will eventually bring him into the haven of salvation."[45] In another place she says, "Whoever halts not in the way of prayer arrives sooner or later."[46] And elsewhere she writes, "that it is on this account that the devil labors so hard to withdraw souls from prayer, because he well knows that he has missed gaining those who faithfully persevere in prayer." Oh, how great are the benefits that flow from prayer! In prayer we conceive holy thoughts, we practice devout affections, we excite great desires, and form efficacious resolutions to give ourselves wholly to God; and thus, the soul is led for his sake to sacrifice earthly pleasures and all disorderly appetites. It was said by St. Aloysius Gonzaga: "There will never be much perfection without much prayer." Let him who longs for perfection mark well this notable saying of the saint.

We should not go to prayer to taste the sweetness of divine love; whoever prays from such a motive will lose his time, or at least derive little advantage from it. A person should begin to pray solely to please God, that is, solely to learn what the will of God is in his regard, and to beg of him the help to put it in practice. The Venerable Father Antony Torres said: "To carry the cross without consolation makes souls fly to perfection. Prayer unattended with sensible consolations confers greater fruit on the soul. But pitiable is the poor soul that leaves off prayer, because she finds no relish in it." St. Teresa said: "When a soul leaves off prayer, it is as if she cast herself into hell without any need of devils."[47]

It results, too, from the practice of prayer, that a person constantly thinks of God. "The true lover" (says St. Teresa) "is ever mindful of the beloved one. And hence it follows that persons of prayer are always speaking of God, knowing, as they do, how pleasing it is to God that his lovers should delight in conversing about him, and on the love he bears them, and that thus they should endeavor to enkindle it in others."[48] The same saint wrote: "Jesus Christ is always found present at the conversations of the servants of God, and he is very much gratified to be the subject of their delight."[49]

Prayer, again, creates that desire of retiring into solitude, in order to converse alone with God, and to maintain interior recollection in the discharge of necessary external duties; I say necessary, such as the management of one's family, or of the performance of duties required of us by obedience; because a person of prayer must love solitude, and avoid dissipation in superfluous and useless affairs, otherwise he will lose the spirit of recollection, which is a great means of preserving union with God: My sister, my spouse is a garden enclosed.[50] The soul espoused to Jesus Christ must be a garden closed against all creatures, and must not admit into her heart other thoughts, nor other business, but those of God or for God. Hearts thrown open never become saints. The saints, who have to labor in gaining souls to God, do not lose their recollection in the midst of all their labors, either of preaching, confessing, reconciling enemies, or assisting the sick. The same rule holds good for those who have to apply to study. How many from excessive study, and a desire to become learned, become neither holy nor learned, because true learning consists in the science of the saints; that is to say, in knowing how to love Jesus Christ; whereas, on the contrary, divine love brings with it knowledge and every good: All good things came to me together with her.[51] that is, with holy charity. The Venerable John Berchmans had an extraordinary love for study, but by his great virtue he never allowed study to interfere with his spiritual interests. The Apostle exhorts us: Not to be more wise than it behooves to be wise, but to be wise unto sobriety.[52] A priest especially must have knowledge; he must know things, because he has to instruct others in the divine law: For the lips of the priest shall keep knowledge, and they shall seek the law at his mouth.[53] He must have knowledge, but unto sobriety. He that leaves prayer for study shows that in his study he seeks himself, and not God. He that seeks God leaves study (if it be not necessary), in order not to omit prayer.

Besides, the greatest evil is that without mental prayer we do not pray at all. I have spoken frequently in my spiritual works of the necessity of prayer, and more especially in a little volume entitled, On Prayer, the great Means, etc.; and in the present chapter also I will briefly say a few other things. It will be sufficient then to quote here the opinion of the Venerable Palafox, Bishop of Osma, in his remarks on the letters of St. Teresa: "How can charity last, unless God grant us perseverance? How will the Lord grant us perseverance unless we ask it of him? And how shall we ask it of him except by prayer? Without prayer there is no communication with God for the preservation of virtue."[54] And so it is, because he that neglects mental prayer sees very little into the wants of his soul, he knows little of the dangers of his salvation, of the means to be used in order to overcome temptations; and so, understanding little of the necessity of prayer, he leaves off praying, and will certainly be lost.

Then as regards subjects for meditation, nothing is more useful than to meditate on the Four Last Things—death, judgment, hell, and heaven; but it is of especial advantage to meditate on death, and to imagine ourselves expiring on the bed of sickness, with the crucifix in our hands, and on the point of entering eternity. But above all, to one that loves Jesus Christ, and is anxious always to increase in his love, no consideration is more efficacious than that of the Passion of the Redeemer. St. Francis de Sales calls "Mount Calvary the mountain of lovers." All the lovers of Jesus Christ love to abide on this mountain, where no air is breathed but the air of divine love. When we see a God dying for our love and dying in order to gain our love (He loved us and delivered Himself up for us [55]), it is impossible not to love him ardently. Such darts of love continually issue forth from the wounds of Christ crucified as pierce even hearts of stone. Oh, happy is he who is ever going during this life to the heights of Calvary! O blessed Mount! O lovely Mount! O beloved Mount! and who shall ever leave thee more! A Mount that sends forth flames to enkindle the souls that perseveringly abide upon thee!

4. Frequent Communion.

The fourth means of perfection, and even of perseverance in the grace of God, is frequently to receive the Holy Communion, of which we have already spoken in the Introduction, §II., page 275, where we affirmed that a soul can do nothing more pleasing to Jesus Christ than to receive him often in the Sacrament of the Altar. St. Teresa said: "There is no better help to perfection than frequent Communion: oh, how admirably does the Lord bring such a soul to perfection!" And she adds, that, ordinarily speaking, they who communicate most frequently are found further advanced in perfection; and that there is greater spirituality in those communities where frequent Communion is the custom. For this reason, it is that, as we find declared in a decree of Innocent XI., in 1679, the holy Fathers have so highly extolled, and so much promoted, the practice of frequent and even of daily Communion. Holy Communion, as the Council of Trent tells us, protects us from daily faults, and preserves us from mortal ones. St. Bernard asserts [56] that Communion represses the movements of anger and incontinence, which are the two passions that most frequently and most violently assail us. St. Thomas says,[57] that Communion defeats the suggestions of the devil. And finally, St. John Chrysostom says, that Communion pours into our souls a great inclination to virtue, and a promptitude to practice it; and at the same time imparts to us a great peace, by which the path of perfection is made very sweet and easy to us. Besides, there is no sacrament so capable of kindling the divine love in souls as the Holy Sacrament of the Eucharist, in which Jesus Christ bestows on us his whole self, to unite us all to himself by means of holy love. Wherefore the Venerable Father John of Avila said: "Whoever deters souls from frequent Communion does the work of the devil." Yes, for the devil has a great horror of this sacrament, from which souls derive immense strength to advance in divine love.

But proper preparation is requisite to communicate well the first preparation, or, in other terms, the remote preparation, to be able to go to Communion daily, or several times in the week, is: 1. To keep free from all deliberate affection to sin that is, to sin committed, as we say, with the eyes open. 2. The practice of much mental prayer. 3. The mortification of the senses and of the passions. St. Francis de Sales [58] teaches as follows: "Whoever has overcome the greatest part of his bad inclinations, and has arrived at a notable degree of perfection, can communicate every day." The angelic Doctor St. Thomas says,[59] that anyone who knows by experience that his soul derives an increase of divine love from the Holy Communion may communicate daily. Hence Innocent XI., in the above-mentioned decree, said that the greater or less frequency of Holy Communion must rest on the decision of the confessor who ought to be guided in this matter by the profit which he sees accrue to the souls under his direction. In the next place, the proximate preparation for Communion is that which is made on the morning itself of Communion, for which there is need of at least half an hour of mental prayer.

To reap also more abundant fruit from Communion, we must make a long thanksgiving. Father John of Avila said that the time after communion is "a time to gain treasures of graces." St. Mary Magdalene of Pazzi used to say that no time can be more calculated to inflame us with divine love than the time immediately after our Communion. And St. Teresa says: "After Communion let us be careful not to lose so good an opportunity of negotiating with God. His divine majesty is not accustomed to pay badly for his lodging, if he meets with a good reception."[60]

There are certain pusillanimous souls, who, on being exhorted to communicate more frequently, reply: "But I am not worthy." But, do you not know, that the more you refrain from Communion, the more unworthy you become of it? Because, deprived of Holy Communion, you will have less strength, and will commit many faults. Well, then, obey your director, and be guided by him: faults do not forbid Holy Communion, when they are not committed with full will; besides, among your failings, the greatest is, not to submit to what your spiritual Father says to you.

"But in my past life I was very bad." And I reply that you must know that he who is weakest has most need of the physician and of medicine. Jesus in the Blessed Sacrament is our physician and medicine as well. St. Ambrose said: "I, who am always sinning, have always need of medicine."[61] You will then say, perhaps: "But my confessor does not tell me to communicate oftener." If then, he does not tell you to do so, ask his permission to communicate oftener. Should he deny you, obey him; but in the meantime, make him the request. "It would seem pride." It would be pride if you were to wish to communicate against his will, but not when you ask his consent with humility. This heavenly bread requires hunger. Jesus loves to be de sired, says a devout author; "He thirsts to be thirsted for."[62] And what a thought is this: "To-day I have communicated, and to-morrow I have to communicate." Oh, how such a reflection keeps the soul attentive to avoid all defects and to do the will of God! "But I have no devotion." If you mean sensible devotion, it is not necessary, neither does God always grant it even to his most beloved souls. It is enough for you to have the devotion of a will determined to belong wholly to God, and to make progress in his divine love. John Gerson says,[63] that he who abstains from Communion because he does not feel that devotion which he would like to feel, acts like a man who does not approach the fire because he does not feel warm.

Alas, my God, how many souls, for want of applying themselves to lead a life of greater recollection and more detachment from earthly things, care not to seek Holy Communion! and this is the true cause of their not wishing to communicate more frequently. They are well aware that to be wishing always to appear, to dress with vanity, to be fond of nice eating and drinking, of bodily comforts, of conversations and amusements, does not harmonize with frequent Communion; they know that more prayer is required, more mortification, as well internal as external, more seclusion; and on this account they are ashamed to approach the altar more frequently. Without doubt, such souls are right to refrain from frequent Communion if they find themselves in that unhappy state of lukewarmness; but whoever is called to a more perfect life should lay aside this lukewarmness, if he would not greatly risk his eternal salvation.

It will be found likewise to contribute very much to keep fervor alive in the soul, often to make a spiritual Communion, so much recommended by the Council of Trent,[64] which exhorts all the faithful to practice it. The spiritual Communion, as St. Thomas says,[65] consists in an ardent desire to receive Jesus Christ in the Holy Sacrament; and therefore, the saints were careful to make it several times in the day. The method of making it is this: "My Jesus, I believe that Thou art really present in the Most Holy Sacrament. I love Thee, and I desire Thee; come to my soul. I embrace Thee; and I beseech Thee never to allow me to be separated from Thee again." Or more briefly thus: "My Jesus, come to me; I desire Thee; I embrace Thee; let us remain ever united together." This spiritual Communion maybe practiced several times a day: when we make our prayer, when we make our visit to the Blessed Sacrament, and especially when we attend Mass at the moment of the priests Communion. The Dominican Sister Blessed Angela of the Cross said: "If my confessor had not taught me this method of communicating spiritually several times a day, I should not have trusted myself to live."

5. Prayer.

The fifth and most necessary means for the spiritual life, and for obtaining the love of Jesus Christ, is prayer. In the first place, I say that by this means God convinces us of the great love he bears us. What greater proof of affection can a person give to a friend than to say to him, "My friend, ask anything you like of me, and I will give it you?" Now, this is precisely what our Lord says to us: Ask, and it shall be given you; seek, and you shall find.[66] Wherefore prayer is called all-powerful with God to obtain every blessing: "Prayer, though it is one, can affect all things," as Theodoret says;[67] whoever prays, obtains from God whatever he chooses. The words of David are beautiful: Blessed be God who hath not turned away my prayer, nor his mercy from me.[68] Commenting on this passage, St. Augustine says, "As long as thou see thyself not failing in prayer, be assured that the divine mercy will not fail thee either." And St. John Chrysostom: "We always obtain, even while we are still praying."[69] When we pray to God, he grants us the grace we ask for, even before we have ended our petition. If then we are poor, let us blame only ourselves, since we are poor merely because we wish to be poor, and so we are undeserving of pity. What sympathy can there be for a beggar, who, having a very rich master, and one most desirous to provide him with everything if he will only ask for it, nevertheless chooses still to continue in his poverty sooner than ask for what he wants? "Behold," says the Apostle, "our God is ready to enrich all who call upon him:" Rich unto all that call upon Him.[70]

Humble prayer, then, obtains all from God; but we must be persuaded at the same time, that if it be useful, it is no less necessary for our salvation. It is certain that we absolutely require the divine assistance, to overcome temptations; and sometimes, in certain more violent assaults, the sufficient grace which God gives to all, might possibly enable us to resist them; but on account of our inclination to evil, it will not ordinarily be sufficient, and we shall stand in need of a special grace. Whoever prays obtains this grace; but whoever prays not, obtains it not, and is lost. And this is more especially the case with regard to the grace of final perseverance, of dying in the grace of God, which is the grace absolutely necessary for our salvation, and without which we should be lost forever. St. Augustine [71] says of this grace, that God only bestows it on those who pray. And this is the reason why so few are saved, because few indeed are mindful to beg of God this grace of perseverance.

In fine, the holy Fathers say, that prayer is necessary for us, not merely as a necessity of precept (so that divines say, that he who neglects for a month to recommend to God the affair of his salvation is not exempt from mortal sin), but also as a necessity of means, which is as much as to say, that whoever does not pray cannot possibly be saved. And the reason of it is, in short, because we cannot obtain eternal salvation without the help of divine grace, and this grace Almighty God only accords to those who pray. And because temptations, and the dangers of falling into God's displeasure, continually have set us, so ought our prayers to be continual. Hence St. Thomas declares that continual prayer is necessary for a man to save himself: "Unceasing prayer is necessary to man, that he may enter heaven."[72] And Jesus Christ himself had already said the same thing: We ought always to pray, and not to faint.[73] And afterwards the Apostle: Pray without ceasing.[74] During the interval in which we shall cease to pray, the devil will conquer us. And though the grace of perseverance can in no wise be merited by us, as the Council of Trent teaches us,[75] nevertheless St. Augustine says, "that in a certain sense we can merit it by prayer."[76] The Lord wishes to dispense his grace to us, but he will be entreated first; nay more, as St. Gregory remarks, he wills to be importuned, and in a manner constrained by our prayers: "God wishes to be prayed to, he wishes to be compelled, he wishes to be, as it were, vanquished by our importunity."[77] St. Mary Magdalene of Pazzi said, "that when we ask graces of God, he not only hears us, but in a certain sense thanks us." Yes, because God, as the infinite goodness, in wishing to pour out himself upon others, has, so to speak, an infinite longing to distribute his gifts; but he wishes to be besought hence it follows, that when he sees himself entreated by a soul, he receives so much pleasure, that in a certain sense he thanks that soul for it.

Well, then, if we wish to preserve ourselves in the grace of God till death, we must act the mendicant, and keep our mouths open to beg for God's help, always repeating, "My Jesus, mercy; never let me be separated from Thee; O Lord, come to my aid; My God, assist me!" This was the unceasing prayer of the ancient Fathers of the desert: "Incline unto my aid, O God: O Lord, make haste to help me![78] O Lord, help me, and help me soon; for if Thou delays Thy assistance, I shall fall and perish!" And this above all must be practiced in the moment of temptation; he who acts otherwise is lost.

And let us have great faith in prayer. God has promised to hear him that prays: Ask, and you shall receive.[79] How can we doubt, says St. Augustine, since God has bound himself by express promise, and cannot fail to grant us the favors we ask of him? "By promising he has made himself our debtor."[80] In recommending ourselves to God, we must have a sure confidence that God hears us, and then we shall obtain whatever we want. Behold what Jesus Christ says: All things, whatsoever you ask when ye pray, believe that you shall receive, and they shall come unto you.[81]

"But," someone may say, "I am a sinner, and do not deserve to be heard." But Jesus Christ says: Everyone that asketh, receiveth.[82] Everyone, be he just, or be he a sinner. St. Thomas teaches us that the efficacy of prayer to obtain graces does not depend on our merits, but on the mercy of God, who has promised to hear every one who prays to him.[83] And our Redeemer, in order to re move from us all fear when we pray, said: Amen, amen, I say to you, if you shall ask the Father anything in My name, He will give it you.[84] As though he would say: Sinners, you have no merits of your own to obtain graces, wherefore do in this manner; when you would obtain graces, ask them of my Father in my name; that is, through my merits and through my love; and then ask as many as you choose, and they shall be granted to you. But let us mark well those words, "In My name;" which signify (as St. Thomas explains it), "in the name of the Savior;" or, in other words, that the graces which we ask must be graces which regard our eternal salvation; and consequently we must remark that the promise does not regard temporal favors; these our Lord grants, when they are profitable for our eternal welfare; if they would prove otherwise, he refuses them. So that we should always ask for temporal favors, on condition that they will benefit our soul. But should they be spiritual graces, then they require no condition; but with confidence, and a sure confidence, we should say: "Eternal Father, in the name of Jesus Christ deliver me from this temptation: grant me holy perseverance, grant me Thy love, grant me heaven." We can likewise ask these graces of Jesus Christ in his own name; that is, by his merits, since we have his promise also to this effect: If you shall ask Me anything in My name, that I will do.[85]

And whilst we pray to God, let us not forget to recommend ourselves at the same time to Mary, the dispenser of graces. St. Bernard says, that it is Almighty God who bestows the graces; but he bestows them through the hands of Mary: "Let us seek grace, and let us seek it through Mary; because what she seeks she finds, and cannot be refused."[86] If Mary prays for us, we are safe; for every petition of Mary is heard, and she can never meet with a repulse.

Affections and Prayers.

O Jesus, my love, I am determined to love Thee as much as I can, and I wish to become a saint; and I wish to become a saint for this reason, in order to give Thee pleasure, and to love Thee exceedingly in this life and the next! I can do nothing of myself, but Thou canst do all things; and I know that Thou wishes me to become a saint. I see already that by Thy grace my soul sighs only for Thee and seeks nothing else but Thee. I wish to live no more for myself; Thou desires me to be wholly Thine, and I desire to be wholly Thine. Come, and unite me to Thyself, and Thyself to me. Thou art infinite goodness; Thou art he who hast loved me so much; Thou art, indeed, too loving, and too lovely; how, then, can I love anything but Thee? I prefer Thy love before all the things of this world; Thou art the sole object, the sole end of all my affections. I leave all to be occupied solely in loving Thee, my Redeemer, my Comforter, my hope, my love, and my all. I will not despair of becoming a saint on account of the sins of my past life; for I know, my Jesus, that Thou didst die in order to pardon the truly penitent. I love Thee now with my whole heart, with my whole soul; I love Thee more than myself, and I bewail, above every other evil, ever having had the misfortune to despise Thee, my sovereign good. Now 1 am no longer my own, I am Thine; God of my heart, dispose of me as Thou pleases. In order to please Thee, I accept of all the tribulations Thou mayest choose to send me sickness, sorrow, troubles, ignominies, poverty, persecution, desolation I accept all to please Thee: in like manner I accept of the death Thou hast decreed for me, with all the anguish and crosses which may accompany it: it is enough if Thou grants me the grace to love Thee exceedingly. Lend me Thy assistance; give me strength henceforth to compensate, by my love, for all the bitterness that I have caused Thee in past time, O only love of my soul!

O Queen of Heaven, O Mother of God, O great advocate of sinners, I trust in thee!

CHARITY IS NOT PUFFED UP

HE THAT LOVES JESUS CHRIST IS NOT VAIN OF HIS OWN WORTH, BUT HUMBLES HIMSELF, AND IS GLAD TO BE HUMBLED BY OTHERS

A proud person is like a balloon filled with air, which seems, indeed, great; but whose greatness is nothing more than a little air; which, as soon as the balloon is opened, is quickly dispersed. He who loves God is humble, and is not elated at seeing any worth in himself; because he knows that whatever he possesses is the gift of God, and that of his own he has only nothingness and sin; so that this knowledge of the divine favors bestowed on him humbles him the more; whilst he is conscious of being so unworthy, and yet so favored by God.

St. Teresa says, in speaking of the especial favors she received from God: "God does with me as they do with a house, which, when about to fall, they prop up with supports." When a soul receives a loving visit from God, and feels within herself an unwonted fervor of divine love, accompanied with tears, or with a great tenderness of heart, let her beware of supposing that God so favors her, in reward for some good action; but let her then humble herself the more, concluding that God caresses her in order that she may not forsake him; otherwise, were she to make such favors the subject of vain complacency, imagining herself more privileged, because she receives greater gifts from God than others, such a fault would induce God to deprive her of his favors. Two things are chiefly requisite for the stability of a house—the foundation and the roof; the foundation in us must be humility, in acknowledging ourselves good for nothing, and capable of nothing; and the roof is the divine assistance, in which alone we ought to put all our trust.

Whenever we behold ourselves unusually, favored by God, we must humble ourselves the more. When St. Teresa received any special favor, she used to strive to place before her eyes all the faults she had ever committed; and thus, the Lord received her into closer union with himself: the more a soul confesses herself undeserving of any favors, the more God enriches her with his graces. Thais, who was first a sinner and then a saint, humbled herself so profoundly before God that she dared not even mention his name; so that she had not the courage to say, "My God;" but she said, "My Creator, have mercy on me!"[1] And St. Jerome writes, that in recompense for such humility, she saw a glorious throne prepared for her in heaven. In the life of St. Margaret of Cortona, we read the same thing; that, when our Lord visited her one day with greater tokens of tenderness and love, she exclaimed: "But, O Lord, hast Thou then forgotten what I have been? Is it possible that Thou canst repay all my outrages against Thee with so exquisite sweetness?" And God replied, that when a soul loves him, and cordially repents of having offended him, he forgets all her past infidelities; as, indeed, he formerly spoke by the mouth of Ezechiel: But if the wicked do penance ... I will not remember all his iniquities.[2] And in proof of this, he showed her a high throne, which he had prepared for her in heaven in the midst of the seraphim. Oh, that we could only comprehend the value of humility! A single act of humility is worth more than all the riches of the universe.

It was the saying of St. Teresa, "Think not that thou hast advanced far in perfection, till thou considers thyself the worst of all, and desires to be placed below all." And on this maxim the saint acted, and so have done all the saints; St. Francis of Assisi, St. Mary Magdalene of Pazzi, and the rest, considered themselves the greatest sinners in the world, and were surprised that the earth sheltered them, and did not rather open under their feet to swallow them up alive; and they expressed themselves to this effect with the sincerest conviction, The Venerable Father John of Avila, who, from his earliest infancy had led a holy life, was on his deathbed; and the priest who came to attend him said many sublime things to him, taking him for what indeed he was, a great servant of God and a learned man; but Father Avila thus spoke to him: "Father, I pray you to make the recommendation of my soul, as of the soul of a criminal condemned to death; for such I am." This is the opinion which saints entertain of themselves in life and death.

We, too, must act in this manner, if we would save our souls, and keep ourselves in the grace of God till death, reposing all our confidence in God alone. The proud man relies on his own strength, and falls on that account; but the humble man, by placing all his trust in God alone, stands firm and falls not, however violent and multiplied the temptations may be; for his watchword is: I can do all things in Him that strengthens me.[3] The devil at one time tempts us to presumption, at another time to diffidence; whenever he suggests to us that we are in no danger of falling, then we should tremble the more; for were God but for an instant to withdraw his grace from us, we are lost. When, again, he tempts us to diffidence, then let us turn to God, and thus address him with great confidence: In Thee, O Lord, have I hoped, I shall never be confounded.[4] My God, in Thee I have put all my hopes; I hope never to meet with confusion, nor to be bereft of Thy grace. We ought to exercise ourselves continually, even to the very last moments of our life, in these acts of diffidence in ourselves and of confidence in God, always beseeching God to grant us humility.

But it is not enough, to be humble, to have a lowly opinion of ourselves, and to consider ourselves the miserable beings that we really are the man who is truly humble, says Thomas à Kempis,[5] despises himself, and wishes also to be despised by others. This is what Jesus Christ so earnestly recommends us to practice, after his example: Learn of Me, because I am meek and humble of heart.[6] Whoever styles himself the greatest sinner in the world, and then is angry when others despise him, plainly shows humility of tongue, but not of heart. St. Thomas Aquinas says that a person who resents being slighted may be certain that he is far distant from perfection, even though he should work miracles. The divine Mother sent St. Ignatius of Loyola from heaven to instruct St. Mary Magdalene of Pazzi in humility; and behold the lesson which the saint gave her: "Humility is a gladness at whatever leads us to despise ourselves."[7] Mark well, a gladness; if the feelings are stirred with resentment at the contempt we receive, at least let us be glad in spirit.

And how is it possible for a soul not to love contempt, if she loves Jesus Christ, and beholds how her God was buffeted and spit upon, and how he suffered in his Passion! Then did they spit in His face and buffeted Him; and others struck His face with the palms of their hands.[8] For this purpose our Redeemer wishes us to keep his image exposed on our altars, not indeed representing him in glory, but nailed to the cross, that we might have his ignominies constantly before our eyes; a sight which made the saints rejoice at being vilified in this world. And such was the prayer which St. John of the Cross addressed to Jesus Christ, when he appeared to him with the cross upon his shoulders: "O Lord, let me suffer, and be despised for Thee!"[9] My Lord, on beholding Thee so reviled for my love, I only ask of Thee to let me suffer and be despised for Thy love.

St. Francis de Sales said,[10] "To support injuries is the touchstone of humility and of true virtue." If a person pretending to spirituality practices prayer, frequent Communion, fasts, and mortifies himself, and yet cannot put up with an affront, or a biting word, of what is it a sign? It is a sign that he is a hollow cane, without humility and without virtue. And what indeed can a soul do that loves Jesus Christ, if she is unable to endure a slight for the love of Jesus Christ, who has endured so much for her? Thomas à Kempis, in his golden little book of the Imitation of Christ, writes as follows: "Since you have such an abhorrence of being humbled, it is a sign that you are not dead to the world, have no humility, and that you do not keep God before your eyes. He that has not God before his eyes, is disturbed at every syllable of censure that he hears."[11] Thou canst not endure cuffs and blows for God; endure at least a passing word.

Oh, what surprise and scandal does that person occasion, who communicates often, and then is ready to resent every little word of contempt! On the contrary, what edification does a soul give that answers contempts with words of mildness, spoken to conciliate the offender; or perhaps makes no reply at all, nor complains of it to others, but continues with placid looks, and without showing the least sign of indignation! St. John Chrysostom says, that a meek person is not only serviceable to himself but likewise to others, by the good example he sets them of meekness in bearing contempt: "The meek man is useful to himself and to others.[12] Thomas à Kempis mentions, with regard to this subject, several things in which we should practice humility; he says as follows: "What others say shall command an attentive hearing, and what you say shall be taken no notice of. Others shall make a request and obtain it; you shall ask for something and meet with a refusal. Others shall be magnified in the mouths of men, and on you no one shall bestow a word. Such and such an office shall be conferred on others, but you shall be passed by as unfit for anything. With such like trials the Lord is wont to prove his faithful servant; and to see how far he has learned to overcome himself and to hold his peace. Nature, indeed, will at times not like it; but you will derive immense profit thereby if you support all in silence."[13]

It was a saying of St. Jane of Chantal, that "a person who is truly humble takes occasion from receiving some humiliation to humble himself the more."[14] Yes, for he who is truly humble never supposes himself humbled as much as he deserves. Those who behave in this manner are styled blessed by Jesus Christ. They are not called blessed who are esteemed by the world, who are honored and praised, as noble, as learned, as powerful;

but they who are spoken ill of by the world, who are persecuted and calumniated; for it is for such that a glorious re ward is prepared in heaven, if they only bear all with patience: Blessed are you when they shall revile you and persecute you, and speak all that is evil against you untruly for My sake: be glad and rejoice, for your reward is very great in heaven.[15]

The grand occasion for practicing humility is when we receive correction for some fault from Superiors or from others. Some people resemble the hedgehog: they seem all calmness and meekness as long as they remain untouched; but no sooner does a Superior or a friend touch them, by an observation on something which they have done imperfectly, than they forthwith become all prickles, and answer warmly, that so and so is not true, or that they were right in doing so, or that such a correction is quite uncalled for. In a word, to rebuke them is to become their enemy; they behave like a person who raves at the surgeon for paining them in the cure of their wounds. "He is angry with the surgeon,"[16] writes St. Bernard. "When the virtuous and humble man is corrected for a fault," says St. John Chrysostom, "he grieves for having committed it; the proud man on the other hand, on receiving correction, grieves also; but he grieves that his fault is detected; and on this account he is troubled, gives answers, and is angry with the person who corrects him." This is the golden rule given by St. Philip Neri, to be observed with regard to receiving correction: "Whoever would really become a saint must never excuse himself, although what is laid to his charge be not true."[17] And there is only one case to be excepted from this rule, and that is when self-defense may appear necessary to prevent scandal. Oh, what merit with God has that soul that is wrongfully reprehended, and yet keeps silence, and refrains from defending itself! St. Teresa said: "There are occasions when a soul makes more progress and acquires a greater degree of perfection by refraining from excusing herself than by listening to ten sermons; because by not excusing herself she begins to obtain freedom of spirit, and to be heedless whether the world speaks well or ill of her."[18]

Affections and Prayers.

O Incarnate Word! I entreat Thee, by the merits of Thy holy humility, which led Thee to embrace so many ignominies and injuries for our love, deliver me from all pride, and grant me a share of Thy humility. And what right have I to complain of any affront whatever that may be offered me, after having so often deserved hell? O my Jesus, by the merit of all the scorn and affronts endured for me in Thy Passion, grant me the grace to live and die humbled on this earth, as Thou didst live and die humbled for my sake. For Thy love I would willingly be despised and forsaken by all the world; but without Thee I can do nothing. I love Thee, O my sovereign good; I love Thee, O beloved of my soul! I love Thee; and I hope, through Thee, to fulfil my purpose of suffering all for Thee, —affronts, betrayals, persecutions, afflictions, dryness, and desolation; enough is it for me if Thou dost not forsake me, O sole object of the love of my soul. Suffer me never more to estrange myself from Thee. Enkindle in me the desire to please Thee. Grant me fervor in loving Thee. Give me peace of mind in suffering for Thee. Give me resignation in all contradictions. Have mercy on me. I deserve nothing; but I fix all my hopes in Thee, who hast purchased me with Thine own blood.

And I hope all from thee, too, O my Queen and my Mother Mary, who art the refuge of sinners!

CHARITY IS NOT AMBITIOUS

HE THAT LOVES JESUS CHRIST DESIRES NOTHING BUT JESUS CHRIST

He that loves God does not desire to be esteemed and loved by his fellowmen: the single desire of his heart is to enjoy the favor of Almighty God, who alone forms the object of his love. St. Hilary writes, that all honor paid by the world is the business of the devil.[1] And so it is; for the enemy traffics for hell, when he infects the soul with the desire of esteem; because, by thus laying aside humility, she runs great risks of plunging into every vice. St. James writes, that as God confers his graces with open hands upon the humble, so does he close them against the proud, whom he resists. God resists the proud and gives His grace to the humble.[2] He says he resists the proud, signifying that he does not even listen to their prayers. And certainly, among the acts of pride we may reckon the desire to be honored by men, and self-exaltation at receiving honors from them.

We have a frightful example of this in the history of Brother Justin the Franciscan, who had even risen to a lofty state of contemplation; but because perhaps—and indeed without a perhaps—he nourished within himself a desire of human esteem, behold what befell him. One day Pope Eugenius IV. sent for him; and on account of the great opinion, he had of his sanctity, showed him peculiar marks of honor, embraced him, and made him sit by his side. Such high honors filled Brother Justin full of self-conceit; on which St. John Capistran said to him, "Alas, Brother Justin, thou didst leave us an angel, and thou return a devil!" And in fact, the hapless Brother becoming daily more and more puffed up with arrogance and insisting on being treated according to his own estimate of himself, he at last murdered a brother with a knife; he afterwards became an apostate, and fled into the kingdom of Naples, where he perpetrated other atrocities; and there he died in prison, an apostate to the last.

Hence it is that a certain great servant of God wisely said, that when we hear or read of the fall of some towering cedars of Libanus, of a Solomon, a Tertullian, an Osius, who had all the reputation of saints, it is a sign that they were not given wholly to God; but nourished inwardly some spirit of pride and so fell away. Let us therefore tremble, when we feel arise within us an ambition to appear in public, and to be esteemed by the world; and when the world pays us some tribute of honor, let us beware of taking complacency in it, which might prove the cause of our utter ruin.

Let us especially be on our guard against all ambitious seeking of preference, and sensibility in points of honor. St. Teresa said, "Where punctiliousness prevails, there spirituality will never prevail."[3] Many persons make profession of a spiritual life, but they are worshippers of self. They have the semblance of certain virtues, but they are ambitious of being praised in all their undertakings; and if nobody else praises them, they praise themselves: in short, they strive to appeal better than others; and if their honor be touched, they lose their peace, they leave off Holy Communion, they omit all their devotions, and find no rest till they imagine they have got back their former standing. The true lovers of God do not so behave. They not only carefully shun every word of self-esteem and all self-complacency, but, further, they are sorry at hearing themselves commended by others, arid their gladness is to behold themselves held in small repute by the rest of men.

The saying of St. Francis of Assisi is most true: "What I am before God, that I am." Of what use is it to pass for great in the eyes of the world, if before God we be vile and worthless? And on- the contrary, what matters it to be despised by the world, provided we be dear and acceptable in the eyes of God? St. Augustine thus writes: "The approbation of him who praises neither heals a bad conscience, nor does the reproach of one who blames wound a good conscience."[4] As the man who praises us cannot deliver us from the chastisement of our evil doings, so neither can he who blames us rob us of the merit of our good actions. "What does it matter," says St. Teresa, "though we be condemned and reviled by creatures, if before Thee, O God! we are great and without blame?" The saints had no other desire than to live unknown, and to pass for contemptible in the estimation of all. Thus writes St. Francis de Sales: "But what wrong do we suffer when people have a bad opinion of us, since we ought to have such of ourselves? Perhaps we know that we are bad, and yet wish to pass off for good in the estimation of others."[5]

Oh, what security is found in the hidden life for such as wish cordially to love Jesus Christ! Jesus Christ himself set us the example, by living hidden and despised for thirty years in a workshop. And with the same view of escaping the esteem of men, the saints went and hid themselves in deserts and in caves. It was said by St. Vincent of Paul,[6] that a love of appearing in public, and of being spoken of in terms of praise, and of hearing our conduct commended, or that people should say that we succeed admirably and work wonders, is an evil which, while it makes us unmindful of God, contaminates our best actions, and proves the most fatal drawback to the spiritual life.

Whoever, therefore, would make progress in the love of Jesus Christ, must absolutely give a deathblow to the love of self-esteem. But how shall we inflict this blow? Behold how St. Mary Magdalene of Pazzi instructs us: "That which, keeps alive the appetite for self-esteem is the occupying a favorable position in the minds of all; consequently, the death of self-esteem is to keep oneself hidden, so as not to be known to anyone. And till we learn to die in this manner, we shall never be true servants of God."[7]

In order, then, to be pleasing in the sight of God, we must avoid all ambition of appearing and of making a parade in the eyes of men. And we must shun with still greater caution the ambition of governing others. Sooner than behold this accursed ambition set foot in the convent, St. Teresa [8] declared she would prefer to have the whole convent burned, and all the nuns with it. So that she signified her wish, that if ever one of her religious should be caught aiming at the Superiorship, she should be expelled from the community, or at least undergo perpetual confinement. St. Mary Magdalene of Pazzi said, "The honor of a spiritual person consists in being put below all, and in abhorring all superiority over others. The ambition of a soul that loves God should be to excel all others in humility, according to the counsel of St. Paul: In humility let each esteem others better than themselves."[9] In a word, he that loves God must make God the sole object of his ambition.

Affections and Prayers.

My Jesus, grant me the ambition of pleasing Thee, and make me forget all creatures and myself also. What will it profit me to be loved by the whole world, if I be not loved by Thee, the only love of my soul! My Jesus, Thou earnest into the world to win our hearts; if I am unable to give Thee my heart, do Thou please to take it and replenish it with Thy love, and never allow me to be separated from Thee any more. I have, alas! turned my back upon Thee in the past; but now that I am conscious of the evil I have done, I grieve over it with my whole heart, and no affliction in the world can so distress me, as the remembrance of the offences that I have so often committed against Thee. I am consoled to think that Thou art infinite goodness, that Thou dost not disdain to love a sinner who loves Thee. My beloved Redeemer, O sweetest love of my soul, I have heretofore slighted Thee; but now at least I love Thee more than myself! I offer Thee myself and all that belongs to me. I have only one wish to love Thee, and to please Thee. This forms all my ambition; accept it, and be pleased to increase it, and exterminate in me all desire of earthly goods. Thou art indeed deserving of love, and great indeed are my obligations of loving Thee. Behold me then, I wish to be wholly Thine; and I will suffer whatever Thou pleases, Thou who for love of me didst die of sorrow on the cross! Thou wish me to be a saint; Thou can make me a saint; in Thee I place my trust.

And I also confide in thy protection, O Mary, great Mother of God!

CHARITY SEEKS NOT HER OWN

HE THAT LOVETH JESUS CHRIST SEEKS TO DETACH HIMSELF FROM EVERY CREATURE

Whoever desires to love Jesus Christ with his whole heart must banish from his heart all that is not God but is merely self-love. This is the meaning of those words, "seeketh not her own;" not to seek ourselves, but only what pleases God. And this is what God requires of us all, when he says: Thou shalt love the Lord thy God with thy whole heart.[1] Two things are needful to love God with our whole heart: 1. To clear it of earth. 2. To fill it with holy love. It follows, that a heart in which any earthly affections linger can never belong wholly to God. St. Philip Neri [2] said, "that as much love as we bestow on the creature, is so much taken from the Creator." In the next place, how must the earth be purged away from the heart? Truly by mortification and detachment from creatures. Some souls complain that they seek God, and do not find him; let them listen to what St. Teresa says: "Wean your heart from creatures, and seek God, and you will find him."[3]

The mistake is, that some indeed wish to become saints, but after their own fashion; they would love Jesus Christ, but in their own way, without forsaking those diversions, that vanity of dress, those delicacies in food: they love God, but if they do not succeed in obtaining such or such an office, they live discontented; if, too, they happen to be touched in point of esteem, they are all on fire; if they do not recover from an illness, they lose all patience. They love God; but they refuse to let go that attachment for the riches, the honors of the world, for the vainglory of being reckoned of good family, of great learning, and better than others. Such as these practice prayer, and frequent Holy Communion;

but because they take with them hearts full of earth, they derive little profit. Our Lord does not even speak to them, for he knows that it is but a waste of words. In fact, he said as much to St. Teresa on a certain occasion: "I would speak to many souls, but the world keeps up such a noise about their ears, that my voice would never be heard by them. Oh, that they would retire a little from the world!" Whosoever, then, is full of earthly affections cannot even so much as hear the voice of God that speaks to him. But unhappy the man that continues attached to the sensible goods of this earth; he may easily become so blinded by them as one day to quit the love of Jesus Christ; and for want of forsaking these transitory goods he may lose God, the infinite good, forever. St. Teresa said: "It is a reasonable consequence, that he who runs after perishable goods should himself perish."

St. Augustine [4] informs us that Tiberius Cæsar desired that the Roman senate should enroll Jesus Christ among the rest of their gods; but the senate refused to do so, on the ground that he was too proud a God and would be worshipped alone without any companions. It is quite true: God will be alone the object of our adoration and love; not indeed from pride, but because it is his just due, and because too of the love he bears us. For as he himself loves us exceedingly, he desires in return all our love; and is therefore jealous of anyone else sharing the affections of our hearts, of which he desires to be the sole possessor: "Jesus is a jealous lover,"[5] says St. Jerome; and he is unwilling therefore for us to fix our affections on anything but himself. And whenever he beholds any created object taking a share of our hearts, he looks on it as it were with jealousy, as the Apostle St. James says, because he will not endure a rival, but will remain the sole object of all our love: Do you think that the Scripture saith in vain: To envy doth the Spirit covet which dwelleth in you?[6] The Lord in the sacred Canticles praises his spouse, saying: My sister, my spouse, is a garden enclosed.[7] He call her "a garden enclosed," because the soul that is his spouse keeps her heart shut against every earthly love, in order to preserve all for Jesus Christ alone. And does Jesus Christ perchance not deserve all our love? Ah, too much, too much has he deserved it, both for his own goodness and for his love towards us. The saints knew this well, and for this reason St. Francis de Sales said: "Were I conscious of one fiber in my heart that did not belong to God, I would forthwith tear it out."[8]

David longed to have wings free from all lime of worldly affections, in order to fly away and repose in God: Who will give me wings like a dove, and I will fly and be at rest?[9] Many souls would wish to see themselves released from every earthly trammel to fly to God, and would in reality make lofty flights in the way of sanctity, if they would but detach themselves from everything in this world; but whereas they retain some little inordinate affection, and will not use violence with themselves to get rid of it, they remain always languishing on in their misery, without ever so much as lifting a foot from the ground. St. John of the Cross said: "The soul that remains with her affections attached to anything, however small, will, notwithstanding many virtues which she may possess, never arrive at divine union; for it signifies little whether the bird be tied by a slight thread or a thick one; since, however slight it may be, provided she does not break it, she remains always bound, and unable to fly. Oh, what a pitiful thing it is to see certain souls, rich in spiritual exercises, in virtues and divine favors; yet, because they are not bold enough to break off some trifling attachment, they cannot attain to divine union, for which it only needed one strong and resolute flight to break effectually that fatal thread! Since, when once the soul is emptied of all affection to creatures, God cannot help communicating himself wholly to her."[10]

He who would possess God entirely must give himself up entirely to God: My beloved to me and I to him,[11] says the Sacred Spouse. My beloved has given himself entirely to me, and I give myself entirely to him. The love which Jesus Christ bears us causes him to desire all our love; and without all he is not satisfied. On this account we find St. Teresa thus writing to the Prioress of one of her convents: "Endeavor to train souls to a total detachment from everything created, because they are to be trained for the spouses of a king so jealous, that he would have them even forget themselves." St. Mary Magdalene of Pazzi took a little book of devotion from one of her novices, merely because she observed that she was too much attached to it. Many souls acquit themselves of the duty of prayer, of visiting the Blessed Sacrament, of frequenting Holy Communion; but nevertheless, they make little or no progress in perfection, and all because they keep some fondness for something in their heart; and if they persist in living thus, they will not only be always miserable, but run the risk of losing all.

We must, therefore, beseech Almighty God, with David, to rid our heart of all earthly attachments: Create a clean heart in me, O God.[12] Otherwise we can never be wholly his. He has given us to understand very plainly, that whoever will not renounce everything in this world, cannot be his disciple: Every one of you that doth not renounce all that he possesses cannot be my disciple.[13] For this reason the ancient Fathers of the desert were accustomed first to put this question to any youth who desired to associate himself with them: "Dost thou bring an empty heart, that the Holy Spirit may fill it?" Our Lord said the same thing to St. Gertrude, when she besought him to signify what he wished of her: "I wish nothing else, he said, but to find a heart devoid of creatures."[14] We must therefore say to God with great resolution and courage: O Lord, I prefer Thee to all; to health, to riches, to honors and dignities, to applause, to learning, to consolations, to high hopes, to desires, and even to the very graces and gifts which I may receive of Thee! In short, I prefer Thee to every created good which is not Thee, O my God. Whatever benefit Thou grant me, O my God, nothing besides Thyself will satisfy me. I desire Thee alone, and nothing else.

When the heart is detached from creatures, divine love immediately enters and fills it. Moreover, St. Teresa said: "As soon as evil occasions are removed, the heart forthwith turns herself to love God." Yes, for the human heart cannot exist without loving; it must either love the Creator or creatures: if it does not love creatures, then assuredly it will love God. In short, we must leave all to gain all. "All for all,"[15] says Thomas à Kempis. As long as St. Teresa cherished a certain affection, though pure, towards one of her relatives, she did not wholly belong to God; but when afterwards she summoned courage, and resolutely cut off the attachment, then she deserved to hear these words from Jesus: "Now, Teresa, thou art all mine, and I am all thine."[16] One heart is quite too small to love this God, so loving and so lovely, and who merits an infinite love; and shall we then think of dividing this one little heart between creatures and God? The Venerable Louis da Ponte felt ashamed to speak thus to God: "O Lord, I love Thee above all things, above riches, honors, friends, relatives;" for it seemed to him as much as to say: "O Lord, I love Thee more than dirt, than smoke, and the worms of the earth! "

The Prophet Jeremias says that the Lord is all goodness towards him who seeks him: The Lord is good to the soul that seek him.[17] But he understands it of a soul that seeks God alone. O blessed loss! O blessed gain! to lose worldly goods, which cannot satisfy the heart and are soon gone, to obtain the sovereign and eternal good, which is God! It is related that a pious hermit, one day while the king was hunting through the wood, began to run to and fro as if in search of something; the king, observing him thus occupied, inquired of him who he was and what he was doing; the hermit replied: "And may I ask your majesty what you are engaged about in this desert?" The king made answer: "I am going in pursuit of game." And the hermit replied: "I, too, am going in pursuit of God." With these words he continued his road and went away. During the present life this must likewise be our only thought, our only purpose, to go in search of God to love him, and in search of his will to fulfil it, ridding our heart of all love of creatures. And whenever some worldly good would present itself to our imaginations to solicit our love, let us be ready prepared with this answer: "I have despised the kingdom of this world, and all the charms of this life, for the sake of the love of my Lord Jesus Christ."[18] And what else are all the dignities and grandeurs of this world but smoke, filth, and vanity, which all disappear at death? Blessed he who can say: "My Jesus, I have left all for Thy love; Thou art my only love; Thou alone art sufficient for me."

Ah, when once the love of God takes full possession of a soul, she of her own accord (supposing always, of course, the assistance of divine grace) strives to divest herself of everything that could prove a hindrance to her belonging wholly to God. St. Francis de Sales remarks that when a house catches fire, all the furniture is thrown out of the window;[19] meaning thereby, that when a person gives himself entirely to God, he needs no persuasion of preachers or confessors, but of his own accord seeks to get rid of every earthly affection. Father Segneri the younger called divine love a robber, which happily despoils us of all, that we may come into possession of God alone. A certain man, of respectable position in life, having renounced everything to become poor for the love of Jesus Christ, was questioned by a friend how he fell into such a state of poverty; he took from his pocket a small volume of the Gospels, and said: "Behold, this is what has stripped me of all." The Holy Spirit says: If a man shall give all the substance of his house for love, he shall despise it as nothing.[20] And when a soul fixes her whole love in God, she despises all, wealth, pleasures, dignities, territories, kingdoms, and all her longing is after God alone; she says, again and again: "My God, I wish for Thee only, and nothing more." St. Francis de Sales writes:[21] "The pure love of God consumes everything which is not God, to convert all into itself; for whatever we do for the love of God is love."

The Sacred Spouse said: He brought me into the cellar of wine, he set in order charity in me.[22] This cellar of wine, writes St. Teresa, is divine love, which, on taking possession of a soul, so perfectly inebriates it as to make it forgetful of everything created. A person intoxicated is, as it were, dead in his senses; he does not see, nor hear, nor speak; and so it happens to the soul inebriated with divine love. She has no longer any sense of the things of the world; she wishes to think only of God, to speak only of God; she recognizes no other motive in all her actions but to love and to please God. In the sacred Canticles the Lord forbids them to awake his beloved, who sleeps: Stir not up, nor make the beloved to awake, till she please.[23] This blessed sleep, enjoyed by souls espoused to Jesus Christ, says St. Basil, is nothing else than "the utter oblivion of all things,"[24] a virtuous and voluntary forgetfulness of every created thing, in order to be occupied solely with God, and to be able to exclaim with St. Francis, "My God and my all."[25] My God, what are riches, and dignities, and goods of the world, compared with Thee! Thou art my all and my every good. "My God and my all." Thomas à Kempis writes,[26] "Oh, sweet word! It speaks enough for him who understands it; and to him who loves, it is most delicious to repeat again and again: My God and my all, my God and my all!"

Detachment from Relatives, above all, regarding one's Vocation

Wherefore, to arrive at perfect union with God, a total detachment from creatures is of absolute necessity. And to come to particulars, we must divest ourselves of all inordinate affection towards relatives. Jesus Christ says: If any man come to Me and hate not his father and mother, and wife and children, and brethren and sisters, yea, and his own life also, he cannot be My disciple.[27] And wherefore this hatred to relatives? because generally, as regards the interests of the soul, we cannot have greater enemies than our own kindred: And a man's enemies shall be those of his own household.[28] St. Charles Borromeo declared that he never went to pay a visit to his family without returning cooled in fervor. And when Father Antony Mendoza was asked why he refused to enter the house of his parents, he replied, "Because I know, by experience, that nowhere is the devotion of religion so dissipated as in the house of parents."

When, moreover, the choice of a state of life is concerned, it is certain that we are not obliged to obey our parents, according to the doctrine of St. Thomas Aquinas.[29] Should a young man be called to the religious life, and find opposition from his parents, he is bound to obey God, and not his parents, who, as the same St. Thomas says, with a view to their own interests and private ends, stand in the way of our spiritual welfare. "Friends of flesh and blood are oftentimes opposed to our spiritual profit."[30] And they are content, says St. Bernard,[31] to have their children go to eternal perdition, rather than leave home. It is surprising, in this matter, to see some fathers and mothers, even though fearing God, yet so blinded by mistaken fondness, that they use every effort, and exhaust every means, to hinder the vocation of a child who wishes to become a religious. This conduct, however (except in very rare cases), cannot be excused from grievous sin.

But someone may say: What, then, and if such a youth does not become a religious, can he not be saved? Are, then, all who remain in the world castaway? I answer: Those whom God does not call into religion may be saved in the world by fulfilling the duties of their state; but those who are called from the world, and do not obey God, may, indeed, possibly be saved; but they will be saved with difficulty, because they will be deprived of those helps which God had destined for them in religion, and for want of which they will not accomplish their salvation. The theologian Habert writes that he who disobeys his vocation remains in the Church like a member out of joint, and cannot discharge his duty without the greatest pain; and so will hardly effect his salvation. Whence he draws this conclusion: "Although, absolutely speaking, he can be saved, yet he will enter on the way, and employ the means of salvation with difficulty."[32]

The choice of a state of life is compared by Father Lewis of Grenada to the mainspring in a watch: if the mainspring be broken, the whole watch is out of order; and the same holds good with regard to our salvation—if the state of life be out of order, the whole life is out of order too. Alas, how many poor youths have lost their vocation through their parents, and have afterwards come to a bad end, and have themselves proved the ruin of their family! There was a certain youth who lost his religious vocation at the instigation of his father; but in course of time, conceiving a great dislike of this same father, he killed him with his own hand, and was executed for the crime. Another young man, whilst pursuing his studies in the seminary, was also called by God to leave the world; heedless of his vocation, he first left off the devout life he was leading, prayer, Holy Communion, etc.; then he gave himself up to vice; and eventually, as he was one night leaving a house of ill-fame, where he had been, he was murdered by his rival. Several priests ran to the spot, but they found him already dead. And, oh, what a sad catalogue of like examples could I add here!

But to return to our subject. St. Thomas advises those who are called to a more perfect life not to take their parents advice, because they would be their enemies in such a case.[33] And if children are not bound to take the advice of their parents on their vocation, they are under less obligation of asking or waiting for their permission, particularly when they have reason to fear that they would unjustly refuse their consent, or prevent them from fulfilling their designs. St. Thomas of Aquinas, St. Peter of Alcantara, St. Francis Xavier, St. Louis Bertrand, and many others, embraced a religious state without even acquainting their parents.

Sanctity required to enter Holy Orders

Again, it must be observed that as we are very much exposed to be lost when to please our relatives we do not follow the divine vocation, so we also endanger our salvation when not to displease them we embrace the ecclesiastical state without being called to it by God. Now, a true vocation to this sublime dignity is distinguished by three signs, namely—the requisite knowledge, the intention of applying oneself only to God's service, and positive goodness of life. We shall here speak only of this last condition.

The Council of Trent has prescribed to bishops to raise to Holy Orders only those whose irreproachable conduct has been proved.[34] This is a rule that Canon Law had already established.[35] Although this is directly understood of the external proof that the bishop should have in regard to the irreproachable conduct of the aspirants to the priesthood, yet one cannot doubt that the Council requires not only external irreproachableness, but even with greater reason, interior irreproachableness, without which the former would be illusory. The Council also adds that those only are to be admitted to Holy Orders who show themselves worthy by a wise maturity.[36] We, moreover, know that the Council prescribes for this end the keeping of the interstices, that is, of an interval of time between the different degrees of Holy Orders.[37]

St. Thomas gives a reason for such a regulation: it is this, that in receiving Holy Orders one is destined to the most sublime ministry, —that of serving Jesus Christ in the Sacrament of the Altar. Hence the angelic Doctor adds that the sanctity of ecclesiastics ought to surpass that of the religious.[38] He elsewhere explains that sanctity is required not only in those who are ordained, but also in the subject who presents himself to be admitted to Holy Orders, and he shows the difference that exists in this respect between the religious and the ecclesiastical state. For in religion one purifies one's self of one's vices, whilst to receive Holy Orders it is necessary that one has already led a pure and holy life.[39] The holy Doctor also says in another place that the candidates for Holy Orders ought to be raised above the simple faithful by their virtue as well as by the dignity of their functions.[40] And this merit he requires before ordination, for he calls it necessary not only in order to exercise well the ecclesiastical functions, but also to be worthily admitted among the number of the ministers of Jesus Christ.[41] He finally concludes with these words: "In the reception of the Sacrament of Holy Orders, the candidates receive a more abundant outpouring of grace in order thus to be in a position to advance to a higher perfection."[42] By these last words, "to advance to a higher perfection," the saint declares that the grace of the sacrament, far from being useless, will dispose the subject by an increase of strength to obtain still greater merits; but he expresses, at the same time, how necessary it is for the candidate to prepare himself in a state of grace that is sufficient in order that he may be judged worthy of entering the sanctuary.

In my Moral Theology[43] I have given on this point a long dissertation to establish that those cannot be excused from mortal sin who without having been sufficiently tried by a holy life receive a Holy Order; since they raise themselves to this sublime state without a divine vocation; for one cannot regard those as having been called by God who have not yet succeeded in overcoming a bad habit, especially the habit of offending against chastity. And whenever among those one might be found who is disposed by repentance to receive the Sacrament of Penance, he would nevertheless not be in a condition to receive Holy Orders, for in his case there must be more holiness of life manifested during a long trial. Otherwise, the candidate would not be exempt from mortal sin on account of the grave presumption that he wished to intrude into the holy ministry without a vocation. Hence St. Anselm says: "Those who thus thrust themselves into Holy Orders and have in view only their own interests are robbers who arrogate to themselves the grace of God; instead of benediction they would receive God's malediction."[44] As Bishop Abelly remarks, they would expose themselves to the great danger of being lost forever: "Whoever deliberately and without troubling himself whether or not he had a vocation would thrust himself into the priesthood, would without doubt plainly expose himself to eternal perdition."[45] Soto holds the same opinion when he asserts, in speaking of the Sacrament of Holy Orders, that positive sanctity in the candidate is of divine precept: "Assuredly," he says, "this sanctity is not essential to the sacrament, though it is altogether necessary by a divine precept. ... Now, the sanctity that should characterize the candidates to Holy Orders does not consist in the general disposition required for the reception of the other sacraments, and sufficient in order that the sacrament may not be impeded. For, in the Sacrament of Holy Orders, one receives not only grace, but one is raised to a much more sublime state. Hence in the candidates there must be great purity of life and perfect virtue."[46] Thomas Sanchez, Holzmann, the school of Salamanca, are also of the same opinion. Thus, what I have advanced is not only the opinion of one theologian, but it is the common teaching based upon what is taught by St. Thomas.

If anyone receive Holy Orders without having led the requisite good life, not only would he himself commit a mortal sin, but also the bishop who confers them upon him without having been morally certain, by sufficient proofs, of the good conduct of the candidate. The confessor also would be guilty of mortal sin, because he gives absolution to one who, addicted to a bad habit, wishes to be ordained without having given evidence during a considerable time of a positively good life. Finally, parents also sin grievously because, though knowing the wicked conduct of their son, they try to induce him to take Holy Orders in order that afterwards he may become the support of the family. Jesus Christ instituted the ecclesiastical state, not to aid the houses of seculars, but to promote the glory of God and the salvation of souls. Some imagine the ecclesiastical state to be an honorable and remunerative employment or trade; but they deceive themselves. Hence, when parents ask the bishop to ordain one of their children who is ignorant, and whose conduct has been bad, alleging that their family is poor, and that they know not how otherwise to extricate themselves from their embarrassment, the bishop must say to them: This I cannot do; the ecclesiastical state is not established to give assistance to poor families, but to promote the good of the church. They should be sent away without listening to them any longer; for such people ordinarily bring ruin not only upon their own souls, but upon their family and their country.

As for the priests who live with their parents, if they are solicited to occupy themselves less with the functions of their ministry than the interests and advancement of their families, they should answer what Jesus Christ one day said, for our own edification, to his holy mother: Did you not know that I must be about my father's business? [47] I am a priest; my duty it is not to amass wealth and procure honors, nor to govern the house, but to live in retirement, to meditate, to study, and to work for the salvation of souls. When it is absolutely necessary to aid one's family, one ought to do so as much as possible without neglecting one's principal care, which is to apply oneself to one's own sanctification, and that of others.

Detachment from Human Respect and from Self-will

Moreover, anyone that would belong wholly to God must be free of all human respect. Oh, how many souls does this accursed respect keep aloof from God, and even separate them from him forever! For instance, if they hear mention made of some or other of their failings, oh, what do they not do to justify themselves, and to convince the world that it is a calumny! If they perform some good work, how industrious are they to circulate it everywhere! They would have it known to the whole world, to be universally applauded. The saints behave in a very different way: they would rather publish their defects to the whole world, in order to pass in the eyes of all for the miserable creatures which they really are in their own eyes; and, on the contrary, in practicing any act of virtue, they prefer to have God alone know of it; for their only care is to be acceptable to him. It is on this account that so many of them were enchanted with solitude, mindful, as they were, of the words of Jesus Christ: But when thou dost alms, let not thy left hand know what thy right hand doth.[48] And again: But thou, when thou shalt pray, enter into thy chamber; and having shut the door, pray to thy Father in secret.[49]

But of all things, self-detachment is most needful; that is, detachment from self-will. Only once succeed in subduing yourself, and you will easily triumph in every other combat. Vince teipsum, "Conquer thyself," was the maxim which St. Francis Xavier inculcated on all. And Jesus Christ said: If anyone would come after Me, let him deny himself.[50] Behold in small compass all that we need practice to become saints; to deny ourselves, and not to follow our own will: Go not after thy lusts, but turn away from thy own will.[51] And this is the greatest grace, said St. Francis of Assisi, that we can receive from God: the power, namely, to conquer ourselves by denying self-will. St. Bernard writes, that if all men would resist self-will, none would ever be damned: "Let self-will cease, and there will be no hell."[52] The same saint writes, that it is the baneful effect of self-will to contaminate even our good works: "Self-will is a great evil, since it renders thy good works no longer good."[53] As, for instance, were a penitent obstinately bent on mortifying himself, or on fasting, or on taking the discipline against the will of his director; we see that this act of penance, done at the instigation of self-will, becomes very defective.

Unhappy the man that lives the slave of self-will! for he shall have a yearning for many things, and shall not possess them; while, on the other hand, he will be forced to undergo many things distasteful and bitter to his inclinations: From whence are wars and contentions among you? Are they not hence? From your concupiscence, which war in your members? You covet and have not.[54] The first war springs from the appetite for sensual delights. Let us take away the occasion; let us mortify the eyes; let us recommend ourselves to God, and the war will be over. The second war arises from the covetousness of riches: let us cultivate a love of poverty, and this war will cease. The third war has its source in ambitiously seeking after honors: let us love humility and the hidden life, and this war too will be no more. The fourth war, and the most ruinous of all, comes from self-will: let us practice resignation in all things which happen by the will of God, and the war will cease. St. Bernard tells us that whenever we see a person troubled, the origin of his trouble is nothing else but his inability to gratify self-will. "Whence comes disquiet," says the saint, " except that we follow self-will?"[55] Our Blessed Lord once complained of this to St. Mary Magdalene of Pazzi, in these words: "Certain souls desire my Spirit, but after their own fancy; and so they become incapable of receiving it."

We must therefore love God in the way that pleases God, and not that pleases us. God will have the soul divested of all, to be united to himself, and to be replenished with his divine love. St. Teresa [56] writes as follows: "The prayer of union appears to me to be nothing more than to die utterly, as it were, to all things in this world, for the enjoyment of God alone. One thing is certain, that the more completely we empty ourselves of creatures, by detaching ourselves from them for the love of God, the more abundantly will he fill us with himself, and the more closely shall we be united with him." Many spiritual persons would attain to union with God; but then they do not desire the contrarieties which God sends them: they fret at having to suffer from ill-health, from poverty, from affronts; but, for want of resignation, they will never come to a perfect union with God. Let us hear what St. Catharine of Genoa said: "To arrive at union with God, the contrarieties which God sends us are absolutely necessary; his purpose is, to consume in us, by means of them, all irregular movements, both within and without. And hence all contempt, ailments, poverty, temptations, and other trials, are all indispensable, to give us the opportunity of fighting; that so, by the way of victory, we may eventually extinguish all inordinate movements, so as to be no more sensible of them; furthermore, until we begin to find contradictions sweet for God's sake, instead of bitter, we shall never arrive at divine union."

I here subjoin the practice of it, taught by St. John of the Cross. The saint says, that to perfect union, "a thorough mortification of the senses and of the appetites is necessary. On the part of the senses, every single relish that presents itself to them, if it be not purely for the glory of God, should forthwith be rejected for the love of Jesus Christ; for example, should you have a desire to see or hear something in no wise conducive to the greater glory of God, then refrain from it. As to the appetites also, endeavor to force ourselves always to choose the worst, the most disagreeable, or the poorest, without fostering any other wish than to suffer and to be despised."[57]

In a word, he that truly loves Jesus Christ loses all affection for things of earth, and seeks to strip himself of all, to keep himself united with Jesus Christ alone. Jesus is the object of all his desires, Jesus the subject of all his thoughts; for Jesus he continually sighs; in every place, at every time, on every occasion, his sole aim is to give pleasure to Jesus. But to reach this point, we must study unceasingly to rid the heart of every affection which is not for God. And I ask, what is meant by giving the soul entirely to God? It means, first, to shun whatever may be displeasing to God, and to do what is most pleasing to him; secondly, it means to accept unreservedly all that comes from his hands, how hard or disagreeable soever it may be; it means, thirdly, to give the preference in all things to the will of God over our own: this is what is meant by belonging wholly to God.

Affections and Prayers.

Ah, my God and my all! I cannot help feeling that, in spite of all my ingratitude and remissness in Thy service, Thou still invites me to love Thee. Behold me, then; I will resist Thee no longer. I will leave all to be wholly Thine. I will no more live for myself: Thy claims on my love are too strong. My soul is enamored of Thee; my Jesus, it sighs after Thee. And how can I possibly love anything else, after seeing Thee die of sufferings on a cross to save me! how could I behold Thee dead, and exhausted with torments, and not love Thee with my whole heart? Yes, I love Thee indeed with all my soul; and I have no other desire but to love Thee in this life and for all eternity. My love, my hope, my courage, and my consolation, give me strength to be faithful to Thee; grant me light, and make known to me from what I ought to detach myself; supply me too with a strong will to obey Thee in all things. love of my soul! I offer myself, and deliver myself up entirely, to satisfy the desire which Thou hast to unite Thyself to me, that I may be wholly united with Thee, my God and my all. Oh, come then, my Jesus; come and take possession of my whole self, and occupy all my thoughts and all my affections. I renounce all my appetites, all my comforts, and all created things; Thou alone art sufficient for me. Grant me the grace to think only of Thee, to desire only Thee, to seek only Thee, my beloved and my only good!

O Mary, Mother of God, obtain for me holy perseverance!

CHARITY IS NOT PROVOKED TO ANGER

HE THAT LOVES JESUS CHRIST IS NEVER ANGRY WITH HIS NEIGHBOR

The virtue not to be angry at the contrarieties that happen to us is the daughter of meekness. We have already spoken at length of the acts which belong to meekness in preceding chapters; but since this is a virtue which requires to be constantly practiced by everyone living among his fellowmen, we will here make some remarks on the same subject more in particular, and more adapted for practice.

Humility and meekness were the favorite virtues of Jesus Christ; so that he bade his disciples learn of him to be meek and humble: Learn of Me, for I am meek and humble of heart.[1] Our Redeemer was called the Lamb—Behold the Lamb of God[2]—as well in consideration of his having to be offered in sacrifice on the cross for our sins, as in consideration of the meekness exhibited by him during his entire life, but more especially at the time of his Passion. When in the house of Caiphas he received a blow from that servant, who at the same time upbraided him with presumption in those words: Answerest thou the high priest so? Jesus only answered: If I have spoken evil, give testimony of the evil; but if well, why strike thou me?[3] He observed the same invariable meekness of conduct till death. While on the cross, and made the object of universal scorn and blasphemy, he only besought the Eternal Father to forgive them: Father, forgive them; for they know not what they do.[4]

Oh, how dear to Jesus Christ are those meek souls who, in suffering affronts, derisions, calumnies, persecutions, and even chastisement and blows, are not irritated against the person that thus injures or strikes them: The prayer of the meek hath always pleased thee.[5] God is always pleased with the prayers of the meek; that is to say, their prayers are always heard. Heaven is expressly promised to the meek: Blessed are the meek, for they shall possess the land.[6] Father Alvarez said that paradise is the country of those who are despised and persecuted and trodden under foot, Yes, for it is for them that the possession of the eternal kingdom is reserved, and not for the haughty, who are honored and esteemed by the world. David declares that the meek shall not only inherit eternal happiness, but shall likewise enjoy great peace in the present life: The meek shall inherit the land, and shall delight in abundance of peace.[7] It is so, because the saints harbor no malice against those who ill-treat them, but rather love them the more; and the Lord, in reward for their patience, gives them an increase of interior peace. St. Teresa said: "I seem to experience a renewed love towards those persons who speak ill of me."[8] This gave occasion to the Sacred Congregation to say of the saint, that "even affronts themselves supplied her with the food of charity."[9] Offences became a fresh reason for her to love the person who had offended her. No one can have such meekness as this, if he has not a great humility and a low opinion of himself, to consider himself worthy of every kind of contempt; and hence we see, on the contrary, that the proud are always irritable and vindictive, because they have a high conceit of themselves, and esteem themselves worthy of all honor.

Blessed are the dead who die in the Lord.[10] We must, indeed, die in the Lord to be blessed, and to enjoy that blessedness even in the present life: we mean, such happiness as can be had before entering heaven, which, though certainly much below that of heaven, yet far surpasses all the pleasures of sense in this world: And the peace of God, which surpasseth all understanding, keep your hearts;[11] so wrote the Apostle to his disciples. But to gain this peace, even in the midst of affronts and calumnies, we must be dead in the Lord: a dead person, how much soever he may be ill-treated and trampled on by others, resents it not; in like manner, he who is meek, like a dead body, which no longer sees or feels, should endure all the outrages committed against him. Whoever loves Jesus Christ from his heart easily attains to this; because, as he is conformed in all things to his will, he accepts with equal composure and peace of mind prosperous and adverse occurrences, consolations and afflictions, injuries, and courtesies. Such was the conduct of the Apostle; and he says, therefore: I exceedingly abound with joy in all our tribulation.[12] Oh, happy the man who reaches this point of virtue! He enjoys continual peace, which is a treasure precious beyond all other goods of this world. St. Francis de Sales said: "Of what value is the whole universe in comparison with peace of heart?"[13] And, in truth, of what avail are all riches and all the honors of the world to a man that lives in disquiet, and whose heart is not at peace?"

In short, to remain constantly united with Jesus Christ, we must do all with tranquility, and not be troubled at any contradiction that we may encounter. The Lord is not in the earthquake.[14] The Lord does not abide in troubled hearts. Let us listen to the beautiful lessons given on this subject by that master of meekness St. Francis de Sales: "Never put yourself in a passion, nor open the door to anger on any pretext whatever; because, when once it has gained an entrance, it is no longer in our power to banish it, or moderate it, when we wish to do so. The remedies against it are: 1. To check it immediately, by diverting the mind to some other object, and not speaking a word. 2. To imitate the Apostles when they beheld the tempest at sea, and to have recourse to God, to whom it belongs to restore peace to the soul. 3. If you feel that, owing to your weakness, anger has already got footing in your breast, in that case do yourself violence to regain your composure, and then try to make acts of humility and of sweetness towards the person against whom you are irritated; but all this must be done with sweetness and without violence, for it is of the utmost importance not to irritate the wounds."[15] The saint said that he himself was obliged to labor much during his life to overcome two passions which predominated in him, namely, anger and love: to subdue the passion of anger, he avowed it had cost him twenty-two years hard struggle. As to the passion of love, he had succeeded in changing its object, by leaving creatures, and turning all his affections to God. And in this manner the saint acquired so great an interior peace, that it was visible even in his exterior; for he was invariably seen with a serene countenance and a smile on his features.

From whence are wars? ... Are they not from your concupiscence?[16] When we are made angry by some contradiction, we fancy we shall find relief and quiet by giving vent to our anger in actions, or at least in words: but we are mistaken, it is not so; for after having done so, we shall find that we are much more disturbed than before. Whoever desires to persevere in uninterrupted peace, must beware of ever yielding to ill-humor. And whenever anyone feels himself attacked by this ill-humor, he must do his utmost to banish it immediately; and he must not go to rest with it in his heart, but must divert himself from it by the perusal of some book, by singing some devout canticle, or by conversing on some pleasant subject with a friend, The Holy Spirit says: Anger resteth in the bosom of a fool.[17] Anger remains a long time in the heart of fools, who have little love for Jesus Christ; but if by stealth it should ever enter into the hearts of the true lovers of Jesus Christ, it is quickly dislodged, and does not remain. A soul that cordially loves the Redeemer never feels in a bad humor, because, as she desires only what God desires, she has all she wishes for, and consequently is ever tranquil and well-balanced. The divine will tranquillizes her in every misfortune that occurs; and thus, she is always able to observe meekness towards all. But we cannot acquire this meekness without a great love for Jesus Christ. In fact, we know by experience that we are not meeker and gentler towards others, except when we feel an increased tenderness towards Jesus Christ.

But since we cannot constantly experience this tenderness, we must prepare ourselves, in our mental prayer, to bear the crosses that may befall us. This was the practice of the saints; and so they were ever ready to receive with patience and meekness injuries, blows, and chastisements. When we meet with an insult from our neighbor, unless we have frequently trained ourselves beforehand, we shall find it extremely difficult to know what course to take, in order not to yield to the force of anger; in the very moment, our passion will make it ap pear but reasonable for us to retort boldly the audacity of the person who affronts us, but St. John Chrysostom says that it is not the right way to quench the fire which is raging in the mind of our neighbor by the fire of an indignant reply; to do so will only enkindle it the more: "One fire is not extinguished by another."[18]

Someone may say: But why should I use courtesy and gentleness towards an impertinent fellow, that insults me without cause? But St. Francis de Sales replies: "We must practice meekness, not only with reason, but against reason."[19]

We must therefore endeavor, on such occasions, to make a kind answer; and in this way we shall allay the fire: A mild answer breaketh wrath.[20] But when the mind is troubled, the best expedient will be to keep silence. St. Bernard writes: "The eye troubled by anger sees not straight."[21] When the eye is dimmed with passion, it no longer distinguishes between what is and what is not unjust; anger is like a veil drawn over the eyes, so that we can no longer discern betwixt right and wrong; wherefore we must, like St. Francis de Sales, make a compact with our tongue: "I have made a covenant with my tongue," he wrote, "never to speak while my heart is disturbed."

But there are moments when it seems necessary to check insolence with severe words. David said: Be angry, and sin not.[22] Occasions do exist, therefore, when we may be lawfully angry, provided it be without sin. But here is just the matter: speculatively speaking, it seems expedient at times to speak and reply to some people in terms of severity, in order to make an impression on them; but in practice it is very difficult to do this without some fault on our part; so that the sure way is always to admonish, or to reply, with gentleness, and to scrupulously guard against all resentment. St. Francis de Sales said: "I have never been angry without afterwards repenting of it." And when, for some reason or other, we still feel warm, the safest way, as I said before, is to keep silence, and reserve the remonstrance till a more convenient moment, when the heart is cooled down.

We ought particularly to observe this meekness when we are corrected by our Superiors or friends. St. Francis de Sales again writes: "To receive a reprimand willingly, shows that we love the virtue opposed to the fault for which we are corrected; and consequently, this is a great sign of progress in perfection."[23]

We must besides practice meekness towards ourselves. It is a delusion of the devil, to make us consider it a virtue to be angry with ourselves for committing some fault; far from it, it is a trick of the enemy to keep us in a state of trouble, that so we may be unfit for the performance of any good. St. Francis de Sales said: "Hold for certain that all such thoughts as create disquiet are not from God, who is the Prince of peace, but proceed either from the devil, or from self-love, or from the good opinion we have of ourselves. These are the three sources from which all our troubles spring. When, therefore, any thoughts arise which throw us into trouble, we must immediately reject and despise them."[24]

Meekness is also especially necessary when we must correct others. Corrections made with a bitter zeal often do more harm than good, especially when he who must be corrected is himself excited: in such cases the correction should be put off, and we must wait until he is cool. And we ourselves ought no less to refrain from correcting while we are under the influence of ill-temper; for then our admonition will always be accompanied with harshness; and the person in fault, when he sees that he is corrected in such a way, will take no heed of the admonition, considering it the mere effect of passion. This holds good as far as concerns the good of our neighbor; as concerns our personal advantage, let us show how dearly we love Jesus Christ, by patiently and gladly supporting every sort of ill-treatment, injury, and contempt.

Affections and Prayers.

O my despised Jesus, O love, O joy of my soul, Thou hast by Thy example made contempt most acceptable to Thy lovers! I promise Thee, from this day forward, to submit to every affront for the love of Thee, who for love of me didst submit on earth to every species of revilement from men. Do Thou grant me strength to keep this promise. Enable me to know and to perform whatever Thou desires at my hands. My God and my all, I crave no other good than Thyself, who art infinite good! O Thou who takes my interests so much too heart, grant that my only care may be to gratify Thee! Grant that all my thoughts may be occupied in avoiding whatever may offend Thee, and in promoting whatever may contribute to Thy good pleasure. Ward off every occasion that may draw me from Thy love. I strip myself of my liberty and consecrate it entirely to Thy good will. I love Thee, O infinite goodness! I love Thee, O my delight! O Word incarnate, I love Thee more than myself! Take pity on me, and heal whatever wounds remain in my poor soul from its past disloyalties towards Thee. I resign myself wholly into Thy arms, O my Jesus; I will be wholly Thine; I will suffer everything for love of Thee; and I ask of Thee nothing but Thyself! O Holy Virgin and my Mother Mary, I love thee, and I rely on thee; succor me by thy powerful intercession!

9

—— o ——

CHARITY THINKETH NO EVIL, REJOICETH NOT IN INIQUITY, BUT REJOICETH WITH THE TRUTH

HE THAT LOVES JESUS CHRIST ONLY WISHES WHAT JESUS CHRIST WISHES

Charity and truth always go together; so that charity, conscious that God is the only and the true good, detests iniquity, which is directly opposed to the divine will, and takes no satisfaction but in what pleases Almighty God. Hence the soul that loves God is heedless of what people say of it, and only aims at pleasing God. The Blessed Henry Suso said: "That man stands well with God who strives to conform himself to the truth, and for the rest is utterly indifferent to the opinion or treatment of mankind."

As we have already more than once asserted, the sanctity and perfection of a soul consists in renouncement of self and in submission to the will of God; but now it will be well to enter more into detail.

I.

The Necessity of Conforming to the Will of God.

If then, we would become saints, our whole endeavor must be, never to follow our own will, but always the will of God; the substance of all the precepts and divine counsels is comprised in doing and suffering what God wills, and in the manner he wills it. Let us, therefore, entreat the Lord to bestow on us a holy liberty of spirit; liberty of spirit leads us to embrace whatever is pleasing to Jesus Christ, regardless of all feelings of repugnance arising from self-love and human respect. The love of Jesus Christ makes those who love him utterly indifferent; so that all things are alike to them, whether bitter or sweet: they do not wish for anything that pleases themselves, but only for that which is pleasing to God; they employ themselves in little and great things, be they pleasant or unpleasant, with the same peace of mind; it is enough for them if they please God.

St. Augustine says: "Love and do what you like."[1] Whoever really loves God seeks only to please him; and in this is all his pleasure. St. Teresa says: "He that seeks but the gratification of one he loves, is gratified with all that pleases that person. Love in its perfection produces this result; it makes a person heedless of all private interests and self-satisfaction and concentrates all his thoughts on endeavoring to please the person beloved, and to do all he can to honor him himself, and to make him honored by others. O Lord, all our ills come from not keeping our eyes fixed on Thee! Were we solely intent on advancing, we should soon come to the end of our journey; but we fall and stumble a thousand times, and we even lose our way, for want of looking attentively to the right path." Here we may see what the single aim of all our thoughts should be, actions, desires, and of all our prayers, namely, the pleasure of God; our way to perfection must be this, to walk according to the will of God.

God wishes us to love him with our whole heart: Thou shall love the Lord thy God with thy whole heart.[2] That person loves Jesus Christ with his whole heart who says to him with the Apostle: Lord, what wilt Thou have me to do?[3] Lord, signify to me what Thou wilt have me do; for I desire to perform all. And let us be persuaded that whilst we desire what God desires, we desire what is best for ourselves; for assuredly God only wishes what is best for us. St. Vincent of Paul said: "Conformity with the will of God is the treasure of a Christian and the remedy for all evils; since it comprises abnegation of self and union with God and all virtues." In this, then, is all perfection: Lord, what wilt Thou have me to do? Jesus Christ promises us, not a hair of your head shall perish.[4] Which is as much as to say, that the Lord rewards us for every good thought we have of pleasing him, and for every tribulation embraced with patience in conformity to his holy will. St. Teresa said,

"The Lord never sends a trial, without remunerating it with some favor as often as we accept it with resignation."[5]

But our conformity to the divine will must be entire, without any reserve, and constant without withdrawal. In this consists of the height of perfection; and to this (I repeat) all our works, all our desires, and all our prayers ought to tend. Some souls given to prayer, on reading of the ecstasies and raptures of St. Teresa and St. Philip Neri, come to wish to enjoy themselves these supernatural unions. Such wishes must be banished as contrary to humility; if we really desire to be saints, we must aspire after true union with God, which is to unite our will entirely to the will of God. St. Teresa [6] said, "Those persons are deceived who fancy that union with God consists in ecstasies, raptures, and sensible enjoyments of him. It consists in nothing else than in submitting our will to the will of God; and this submission is perfect when our will is detached from everything, and so completely united with that of God, that all its movements depend solely on the will of God. This is the real and essential union which I have always sought after, and continually beg of the Lord." And then she adds: "Oh, how many of us say this, and seem to ourselves to desire nothing besides this; but, miserable creatures that we are, how few of us attain it!" Such, indeed, is the undeniable truth; many of us say: O Lord! I give Thee my will, I desire nothing but what Thou desires; but, in the event of some trying occurrence, we are at a loss how to yield calmly to the divine will. And this is the source of our continual complaint that we are unfortunate in the world, and that we are the butt of every misfortune, and so of our dragging on an unhappy life.

If we were conformed to the divine will in every trouble, we should undoubtedly become saints, and be the happiest of mankind. This, then, should form the chief object of our attention, to keep our will in unbroken union with the will of God in every occurrence of life, be it pleasant or unpleasant. It is the admonition of the Holy Spirit. Winnow not with every wind.[7] Some people resemble the weathercocks, which turn about every wind that blows; if the wind is fair and favorable to their desires, they are all gladness and condescension; but if there blow a contrary wind, and things fall out against their desires, they are all sadness and impatience; this is why they do not become saints, and why their life is unhappy, because, in the present life, adversity will always befall us in a greater measure than prosperity. St. Dorotheus said, that to receive from the hands of God whatever happens is a great means to keep ourselves in continual peace and tranquility of soul. And the saint relates, that on this account the ancient Fathers of the desert were never seen angry or melancholy, because they accepted whatever happened to them joyfully, as coming from the hands of God. Oh, happy the man who lives wholly united and abandoned to the divine will! he is neither puffed up by success nor depressed by reverses; for he well knows that all alike comes from the self-same hand of God; the will of God is the single rule of his own will; thus he only does what God wishes him to do, and he only desires what God does. He is not anxious to do many things, but to accomplish with perfection what he knows to be acceptable to God. Accordingly, he prefers the minutest obligations of his state of life to the most glorious and important actions, well aware that in the latter self-love may find a great share, whereas in the former there is certainly the will of God.

Thus we, too, shall be happy when we receive from God all the dispositions of his Providence in the spirit of perfect conformity to his divine will, utterly regardless of whether or not they coincide with our private inclinations. The saintly Mother de Chantal said: "When shall we come to relish the divine will in every event that happens, without paying attention to anything else but the good pleasure of God, from whom it is certain that prosperity and adversity proceed alike from motives of love and for our best interests? When shall we resign ourselves unreservedly into the arms of our most loving heavenly Father, entrusting him with the care of our persons and our affairs, and reserving nothing for ourselves but the sole desire of pleasing God?" The friends of St. Vincent of Paul said of him while he was still on earth: "Vincent is always Vincent." By which they meant to say, that the saint was ever to be seen with the same smiling face, whether in prosperity or in adversity; and was always himself, because, as he lived in the total abandonment of himself to God, he feared nothing and desired nothing but what was pleasing to God. St. Teresa said: "By this holy abandonment that admirable liberty of spirit is generated, which those who are perfect possess, wherein they find all the happiness in this life which they can possibly desire; inasmuch as, fearful of nothing, and desirous or wanting for nothing in the things of this world, they possess all."[8]

Many, on the other hand, fabricate a sort of sanctity according to their own inclinations; some, inclined to melancholy, make sanctity consist in living in seclusion; others, of a busy temperament, in preaching and in making up quarrels; some, of an austere nature, in penitential inflictions and macerations; others, who are naturally generous, in distributing alms; some in saying many vocal prayers; others in visiting sanctuaries; and all their sanctity consists in such or the like practices. External acts are the fruit of the love of

Jesus Christ; but true love itself consists in a complete conformity to the will of God; and because of this, in denying ourselves and in preferring what is most pleasing to God, and solely because he deserves it.

Others wish to serve God; but it must be in that employment, in that place, with those companions, and in such circumstances; or else they either neglect their duty, or at least do it with a bad grace: such as these are not free in spirit, but are slaves of self-love, and on that account reap little merit even from what they perform; moreover, they live in perpetual disquiet, since their attachment to self-will makes the yoke of Jesus Christ become heavy to them. The true lovers of Jesus Christ love only that which is pleasing to Jesus Christ, and for the sole reason that it does please him; and they love it when it pleases Jesus Christ, where it pleases him, and how it pleases him; whether he chooses to employ them in honorable functions, or in mean and lowly occupations; in a life of notoriety in the world, or in one hidden and despised. This is the real drift of what is meant by the pure love of Jesus Christ; hence we must labor to overcome the cravings of our self-love, which seeks to be employed in those works only that are glorious, or that are according to our own inclinations. And what will it profit us to be the most honored, the wealthiest, the greatest in this world, without the will of God? The Blessed Henry Suso said, "I would rather be the vilest insect on earth by the will of God, than a seraph in heaven by my own will."

Jesus Christ said: Many shall say: Lord, we have cast out devils and done great wonders in Thy name: Lord, have we not prophesied in Thy name, and cast out devils in Thy name, and done many miracles in Thy name.[9] But the Lord will answer them: I never knew you; depart from Me, you that work iniquity.[10] Depart from me; I never acknowledged you for my disciples, because you preferred to follow your own inclinations rather than my will. And this is especially applicable to those priests who labor much for the salvation or perfection of others, while they themselves continue to live on in the mire of their imperfections. Perfection consists of: First, in a true contempt of oneself. Secondly, in a thorough mortification of our own appetites. Thirdly, in a perfect conformity to the will of God: whosoever is wanting in one of these virtues is out of the way of perfection. On this account a great servant of God said, it was better for us in our actions to have the will of God rather than his glory as their sole end; for in doing the will of God, we at the same time promote his glory; whereas in proposing to ourselves the glory of God, we frequently deceive ourselves, and follow our own will under pretext of glorifying God. St. Francis de Sales said: "There are many who say to the Lord: I give myself wholly to Thee without reserve; but few indeed, in point of fact, practically embrace this abandonment. It consists in a certain indifference in accepting all kinds of events, just as they fall out according to the order of divine Providence, afflictions as well as consolations, slights, and injuries as well as honor and glory."[11]

It is therefore in suffering, and in embracing with cheerfulness whatever cuts against the grain of our own inclinations, that we can discover who is a true lover of Jesus Christ. Thomas à Kempis says, "that he is not deserving of the name of lover who is not ready to endure all things for his beloved, and to follow in all things the will of his beloved."[12] On the contrary, Father Balthazar Alvarez said, that whoever quietly resigns himself to the divine will in troubles "travels to God post-haste." And the saintly Mother Teresa said: "What greater acquisition can we make, than to have some proof that we are pleasing God?" And to this I add that we cannot have a more certain proof of this, than by peacefully embracing the crosses which God sends us. We please God by thanking him for his benefits on earth; but, says Father John of Avila, one "blessed be God" uttered in adversity is worth six thousand acts of thanksgiving in prosperity.

And here we must observe that we must receive with resignation not merely the crosses which come directly from God; for instance, ill-health, scanty talents, accidental reverses of fortune; but such, moreover, as come indirectly from God, and directly from our fellow-men; for instance, persecutions, thefts, injuries; for all, in reality, come from God. David was one day insulted by one of his vassals called Semei, who not only upbraided him with words of contumely, but even threw stones at him. One of the courtiers would have forthwith avenged the insult by cutting off the head of the offender; but David replied: Let him alone and let him curse; for the Lord hath bid him curse David;[13] or, in other words, God makes use of him to chastise me for my sins, and therefore he allowed him to pursue me with injuries.

Wherefore St. Mary Magdalene of Pazzi said, that all our prayers should have for their end to obtain from God the grace to follow his holy will in all things. Certain souls: greedy of spiritual dainties in prayer, go in search only of these banquets of sweet and tender feelings; but courageous souls that seek sincerely to belong wholly to God, ask him only for light to understand his will, and for strength to put it in execution. To attain to purity of love, it is necessary to submit our will in all things to the will of God: Never consider yourselves," said St. Francis de Sales, "to have arrived at the purity which you ought to have, as long as your will is not cheerfully obedient, even in things the most repulsive, to the will of God." "Because," as St. Teresa remarks, "the giving up of our will to God draws him to unite himself to our lowliness."[14] But this can never be obtained, except by means of mental prayer and of continual petitions addressed to the divine majesty, nor without a cordial desire to belong entirely to Jesus Christ without reserve.

O most amiable Heart of my divine Savior, Heart enamored of mankind, since Thou loves us with such a depth of tenderness; O Heart, in fine, worthy to rule over and possess all our hearts, would that I could make all men comprehend the love Thou barest them, and the tender caresses Thou dost lavish on those who love Thee without reserve! O Jesus my love, be pleased to accept the offering and the sacrifice which I this day make to Thee of my entire will! Acquaint me with what Thou wouldst have me to do; for I am determined to do all by the help of Thy grace.

II.

Obedience.

Now what is the surest way to know and ascertain what God requires of us? There is no surer way than to practice obedience to our Superiors and directors. St. Vincent of Paul said: "The will of God is never better complied with than when we obey our Superiors." The Holy Ghost says: Much better is obedience than the victims of fools.[15] God is more pleased with the sacrifice which we make to him of our own will, by submitting it to obedience, than with all other sacrifices which we can offer him; because in other things, as in alms-deeds, fasting, mortifications, and the like, we give of what is ours to God, but in giving him our will we present him ourselves: when we give him our goods, our mortifications, we give him part; but when we give him our will, we give him everything. So that when we say to God, O Lord, make me know by means of obedience what Thou requires of me, for I wish to comply with all, we have nothing more to offer him.

Whoever, therefore, gives himself up to obedience, must detach himself totally from his own opinion. "What though each one," says St. Francis de Sales, "has his own opinions, virtue is not thereby violated; but virtue is violated by the attachment which we have to our own opinions."[16] But alas! this attachment is the hardest thing to part with; and hence there are so few persons wholly given to God, because few render a thorough submission to obedience. There are some persons so fondly attached to their own opinion, that, on receiving an obedience, although the thing enjoined suit their inclination, yet, from the very fact that it is commanded, they lose all fancy for it, all wish to discharge it; for they find no relish in anything but in following the dictates of their individual will. How different is the conduct of saints! Their only happiness flows from the execution of what obedience imposes on them. The saintly Mother Jane Frances de Chantal once told her daughters that they might spend the recreation-day in any manner they chose. When the evening came, they all went to her, to beg most earnestly that she would never again grant them such permission; for they had never spent such a wearisome day as that on which they had been set free from obedience.

It is a delusion to think that anyone can possibly be better employed than in the discharge of what obedience has imposed. St. Francis de Sales says: "To desert an occupation given by obedience in order to unite ourselves to God by prayer, by reading, or by recollection, would be to withdraw from God to unite ourselves to our own self-love."[17] St. Teresa adds, moreover, that whoever performs any work, even though it be spiritual, yet against obedience, assuredly works by the instigation of the devil, and not by divine inspiration, as he perhaps flatters himself; "because," says the saint, "the inspirations of God always come in company with obedience." To the same effect she says elsewhere; "God requires nothing more of a soul that is determined to love him than obedience."[18] "A work done out of obedience," says Father Rodriguez, "outweighs every other that we can imagine." To lift a straw from the ground out of obedience is of greater merit than a protracted prayer, or a discipline to blood, through our own will. This caused St. Mary Magdalene of Pazzi to say, that she would rather be engaged in some exercise from obedience than in prayer; "because," said she, "in obedience I am certain of the will of God, whereas I am by no means so certain of it in any other exercise."[19] According to all spiritual masters, it is better to leave off any devout exercise through obedience, than to continue it without obedience. The Most Blessed Virgin Mary revealed once to St. Bridget,[20] that he who relinquishes some mortification through obedience reaps a twofold profit; since he has already obtained the merit of the mortification by the goodwill to do it, and he also gains the merit of obedience by foregoing it. One day the famous Father Francis Arias went to see the Venerable Father John of Avila, his intimate friend, and he found him pensive and sad; he asked him the reason, and received this answer: "O happy you, who live under obedience, and are sure of doing the will of God. As for me, who shall warrant me whether I do a thing more pleasing to God in going from village to village, catechizing the poor peasants, or in remaining stationary in the confessional, to hear every one that presents himself? Whereas he that is living under obedience is always sure that whatever he performs by obedience is according to the will of God, or rather that it is what is most acceptable to God." Let this serve as a consolation for all those who live under obedience.

For obedience to be perfect, we must obey with the will and with the judgment. To obey with the will signifies to obey willingly, and not by constraint, after the fashion of slaves; to obey with the judgment means to conform our judgment to that of the Superior, without examining what is commanded. St. Mary Magdalene of Pazzi remarks on this: "Perfect obedience demands a soul without judgment." To the like purpose, St. Philip Neri said that, in order to obey with perfection, it was not enough to execute the thing commanded, but it must be done without reasoning on it; taking it for certain that what is commanded us is for us the most perfect thing we can do, although the opposite might be better before God.[21]

This holds good not merely for religious, but likewise for seculars living under obedience to their spiritual directors. Let them request their director to prescribe them rules for the guidance of their affairs, both spiritual and temporal; and so, they will make sure of doing what is best. St. Philip Neri said: "Let those who are desirous of progressing in the way of God submit themselves to a prudent confessor, whom they should obey as in God's place. By so doing, we are certain of not having to render an account to God of the actions we perform."[22]

He said, moreover, "that we must place faith in the confessor, because the Lord will not permit him to err; that nothing is so sure of cutting off all the snares of the devil as to do the will of others in the performance of good; and that there is nothing more dangerous than to wish to direct ourselves according to our private fancy." In like manner, St. Francis de Sales says, in speaking of the direction of the spiritual Father as a means of walking securely in the path of perfection, "This is the maxim of all maxims."[23] "Seek as you will," says the devout Avila, "you will never so surely find the will of God as in the way of this humble obedience, so much recommended and so practiced by all the ancient servants of God." The same thing is affirmed by St. Bernard, St. Bernardine of Siena, St. Antoninus, St. John of the Cross, St. Teresa, John Gerson, and all theologians and masters of the spiritual life; and St. John of the Cross said, that to call this truth in question is almost to doubt of the faith. The words of the saint are, "not to be satisfied with what the confessor says, is arrogance, and a want of faith."

Among the maxims of St. Francis de Sales are the two following, most consolatory for scrupulous souls: "First, a truly obedient soul was never yet lost; secondly, we ought to be satisfied on being told by our spiritual director that we are going on well, without seeking to be convinced of it ourselves." It is the teaching of many Doctors, as of Gerson, St. Antoninus, Cajetanus, Navarrus, Sanchez, Bonacina, Cordovius, Castropalao, and the Doctors of Salamanca, with others, that the scrupulous person is bound, under strict obligation, to act in opposition to scruples, when from such scruples there is reason to apprehend grievous harm happening to soul or body, such as the loss of health, or of intellect; wherefore scrupulous persons ought to have greater scruple at not obeying the confessor than at acting in opposition to their scruples.

To sum up, therefore, all that has been said in this chapter, our salvation and perfection consist of: 1. In denying ourselves; 2. In following the will of God; 3. In praying to him always to give us strength to do both one and the other.

Affections and Prayers.

What have I in heaven? and besides Thee what do I desire upon earth? Thou art the God of my heart, and the God that is my portion forever.[24] My beloved Redeemer, infinitely amiable, since Thou hast come down from heaven to give Thyself wholly to me, what else shall I seek for on earth or in heaven besides Thee, who art the sovereign good, the only good worthy to be loved? Be Thou, then, the sole Lord of my heart, do Thou possess it entirely: may my soul love Thee alone, obey Thee alone, and seek to please no other than Thee. Let others enjoy the riches of this world, I wish only for Thee: Thou art and shalt ever be my treasure in this life and in eternity Wherefore I give Thee, O my Jesus, my whole heart and all my will. It was at one time, alas! a rebel against Thee; but now I dedicate it wholly to Thee. Lord, what wilt Thou have me to do?[25] Tell me what Thou requires of me and lend me Thy assistance; for I will leave nothing undone. Dispose of me, and of all that concerns me, as Thou pleases; I accept all, and resign myself to all. O Love deserving of infinite love, Thou hast loved me so as even to die for me; I love Thee with my whole heart, I love Thee more "than myself, and into Thy hands I abandon my soul. On this very day I bid farewell to every worldly affection, I take leave of everything created, and I give myself without reserve to Thee; Through the merits of Thy Passion receive me and make me faithful unto death. My Jesus, my Jesus, from this day forward I will live only for Thee, I will love none but Thee, I will seek nothing else than to do Thy blessed will.

Aid me by Thy grace, and aid me, too, by thy protection, O Mary my hope.

CHARITY BEARETH ALL THINGS

HE THAT LOVES JESUS CHRIST BEARS ALL THINGS FOR JESUS CHRIST, AND ESPECIALLY ILLNESSES, POVERTY, AND CONTEMPT

In Chapter I. we spoke of the virtue of patience in general. In this we will speak of certain matters in particular, which demand the especial practice of patience.

Father Balthazar Alvarez [1] said that a Christian need not imagine himself to have made any progress until he has succeeded in penetrating his heart with a lasting sense of the sorrows, poverty, and ignominies of Jesus Christ to support with loving patience every sort of sorrow, privation, and contempt, for the sake of Jesus Christ.

I.

Patience in Sickness.

In the first place, let us speak of bodily infirmities, which, when borne with patience, merit for us a beautiful crown.

St. Vincent de Paul said: "Did we but know how precious a treasure is contained in infirmities, we should accept of them with joy as the greatest possible blessings." Hence the saint himself, though constantly afflicted with ailments, that often left him no rest day or night, bore them with so much peace and such serenity of countenance that no one could guess that anything ailed him at all. Oh, how edifying is it to see a sick person bear his illness with a peaceful countenance, as did St. Francis de Sales! When he was ill, he simply explained his complaint to the physician, obeyed him exactly by taking the prescribed medicines, however nauseous; and for the rest he remained at peace, never uttering a single complaint in all his sufferings. What a contrast to this is the conduct of those who do nothing but complain even for the most trifling indisposition, and who would like to have around them all their relatives and friends to sympathize with them! Far different was the instruction of St. Teresa to her nuns: "My sisters, learn to suffer something for the love of Jesus Christ, without letting all the world know of it."[2] One Good Friday Jesus Christ favored the Venerable Father Louis da Ponte with so much bodily suffering, that no part of him was exempt from its particular pain: he mentioned his severe sufferings to a friend; but he was afterwards so sorry at having done so, that he made a vow never again to reveal to anybody whatever he might afterwards suffer. I say "he was favored;" for, to the saints, the illnesses, and pains which God sends them are real favors. One day St. Francis of Assisi lay on his bed in excruciating torments; a companion said to him: "Father, beg God to ease your pains, and not to lay so heavy a hand upon you." On hearing this, the saint instantly leaped from his bed, and going on his knees, thanked God for his sufferings; then, turning to his companion, he said: "Listen, did I not know that you so spoke from simplicity, I would refuse ever to see you again."[3]

Some one that is sick will say, it is not so much the infirmity itself that afflicts me, as that it disables me from going to church to perform my devotions, to communicate, and to hear Holy Mass; I cannot go to choir to recite the divine Office with my brethren; I cannot celebrate Mass; I cannot pray; for my head is aching with pain, and is light almost to fainting. But tell me now, if you please, why do you wish to go to church or to choir? Why would you communicate and say or hear Holy Mass? is it to please God? but it is not now the pleasure of God that you say the Office, that you communicate, or hear Mass; but that you remain patiently on this bed and support the pains of this infirmity. But you are displeased with my speaking; thus, then you are not seeking to do what is pleasing to God, but what is pleasing to yourself. The Venerable John of Avila wrote as follows to a priest who so complained to him: "My friend, busy not yourself with what you would do if you were well but be content to remain ill as long as God thinks fit. If you seek the will of God, what matters it to you whether you be well or ill?"[4]

You say you are unable even to pray because your head is weak. Be it so: you cannot meditate; but why cannot you make acts of resignation to the will of God? If you would only make these acts, you could not make a better prayer, welcoming with love all the torments that assail you. So did St. Vincent of Paul: when attacked by a serious illness, he was wont to keep himself tranquilly in the presence of God, without forcing his mind to dwell on any particular subject; his sole exercise was to elicit some short acts from time to time, as of love, of confidence, of thanksgiving, and more frequently of resignation, especially in the crisis of his sufferings. St. Francis de Sales made this remark: "Considered in themselves, tribulations are terrifying; but considered in the will of God, they are lovely and delightful."[5] You cannot say prayers; and what more exquisite prayer than to cast a look from time to time on your crucified Lord, and to offer him your pains, uniting the little that you endure to the overwhelming torments that afflicted Jesus on the cross!

There was a certain pious lady lying bedridden with many disorders; and on the servant putting the crucifix into her hand, and telling her to pray to God to deliver her from her miseries, she made answer: "But how can you desire me to seek to descend from the cross, whilst I hold in my hand a God crucified? God forbid that I should do so. I will suffer for him who chose to suffer torments for me incomparably greater than mine." This was, indeed, precisely what Jesus Christ said to St. Teresa when she was laboring under serious illness; he appeared to her all covered with wounds, and then said to her: "Behold, my daughter, the bitterness of my sufferings, and consider if yours equal mine."[6] Hence the saint was accustomed to say, in the midst of all her infirmities: "When I remember in how many ways my Savior suffered, though he was innocence itself, I know not how it could enter my head to complain of my sufferings." During a period of thirty-eight years, St. Lidwine was afflicted with numberless evils fevers, gout in the feet and hands, and sores, all her lifetime; nevertheless, from never losing sight of the sufferings of Jesus Christ, she maintained an unbroken cheerfulness and joy. In like manner, St. Joseph of Leonessa, a Capuchin, when the surgeon was about to amputate his arm, and his brethren would have bound him, to prevent him from stirring through vehemence of pain, seized hold of the crucifix and exclaimed: "Wherefore bind me?—wherefore bind me? behold who it is that binds me to support every suffering patiently for love of him;" and so he bore the operation without a murmur. St. Jonas the Martyr, after passing the entire night immersed in ice by order of the tyrant, declared next morning that he had never spent a happier night, because he had pictured to himself Jesus hanging on the cross; and thus, compared with the torments of Jesus, his own had seemed rather caresses than torments.

Oh, what abundance of merits may be accumulated by patiently enduring illnesses! Almighty God revealed to Father Balthazar Alvarez the great glory he had in store for a certain nun, who had borne a painful sickness with resignation; and told him that she had acquired greater merit in those eight months of her illness than some other religious in many years. It is by the patient endurance of ill-health that we weave a great part, and perhaps the greater part, of the crown that God destines for us in heaven. St. Lidwine had a revelation to this effect. After sustaining many and most cruel disorders, as we mentioned above, she prayed to die a martyr for the love of Jesus Christ; now as she was one day sighing after this martyrdom, she suddenly saw a beautiful crown, but still incomplete, and she understood that it was destined for herself; whereupon the saint, longing to behold it completed, entreated the Lord to increase her sufferings. Her prayer was heard, for some soldiers came shortly after, and ill-treated her, not only with injurious words, but with blows and outrage. An angel then appeared to her with the crown completed and informed her that those last injuries had added to it the gems that were wanting; and shortly afterwards she expired.

Ah, yes! to the hearts that fervently love Jesus Christ, pains and ignominies are most delightful. And thus, we see the holy martyrs going with gladness to encounter the sharp prongs and hooks of iron, the plates of glowing steel and axes. The martyr St. Procopius thus spoke to the tyrant who tortured him: "Torment me as you like; but know at the same time, that nothing is sweeter to the lover of Jesus Christ than to suffer for his sake."[7] St. Gordius, Martyr, replied in the same way to the tyrant who threatened him death: "Thou threatenest me with death; but I am only sorry that I cannot die more than once for my own beloved Jesus."[8] And I ask. did these saints speak thus because they were insensible to pain or weak in intellect? "No," replies St. Bernard; "not insensibility, but love caused this."[9] They were not insensible, for they felt well enough the torments inflicted on them; but since they loved God, they esteemed it a great privilege to suffer for God, and to lose all, even life itself, for the love of God.

Above all, in time of sickness we should be ready to accept of death, and of that death which God pleases. We must die, and our life must finish in our last illness; nor do we know which will be our last illness. Where fore in every illness we must be prepared to accept that death which God has appointed for us. A sick person says: "Yes; but I have committed many sins and have done no penance. I should like to live, not for the sake of living, but to make some satisfaction to God before my death." But tell me, my brother, how do you know that if you live longer you will do penance, and not rather do worse than before? At present you can well cherish the hope that God has pardoned you; what penance can be more satisfactory than to accept of death with resignation, if God so wills it? St. Aloysius Gonzaga, at the age of twenty-three, gladly embraced death with this reflection: "At present," he said, "I am, as I hope, in the grace of God. Hereafter, I know not what may befall me; so that I now die contentedly, if God calls me to the next life."[10] It was the opinion of Father John of Avila that every one, provided he be in good dispositions, though only moderately good, should desire death, to escape the danger, which always surrounds us in this world, of possibly sinning and losing the grace of God.

Besides, owing to our natural frailty, we cannot live in this world without committing at least venial sins; this should be a motive for us to embrace death willingly, that we may never offend God anymore. Further, if we truly love God, we should ardently long to go to see him, and love him with all our strength in Paradise, which no one can do perfectly in this present life; but unless death open us the door, we cannot enter that blessed region of love. This caused St. Augustine, that loving soul, to cry out: "Oh, let me die, Lord, that I may behold Thee!"[11] O Lord, let me die, otherwise I cannot behold and love Thee face to face.

II.

Patience in Poverty.

In the second place, we must practice patience in the endurance of poverty. Our patience is certainly very much tried when we need temporal goods. St. Augustine said: "He that has not God, has nothing; he that has God, has all."[12] He who possesses God, and remains united to his blessed will, finds every good. Witness St. Francis, barefooted, clad in sackcloth, and deprived of all things, yet happier than all the monarchs of the world, by simply repeating, "My God and my all."[13] A poor man is properly he that has not what he desires; but he those desires nothing, and is contented with his poverty, is in fact very rich. Of such St. Paul says: Having nothing yet possessing all things.[14] The true lovers of God have nothing, and yet have everything; since, when temporal goods fail them, they exclaim: "My Jesus, Thou alone art sufficient for me;" and with this they rest satisfied. Not only did the saints maintain patience in poverty, but sought to be despoiled of all, to live detached from all, and united with God alone. If we have not courage enough to renounce all worldly goods, at all events let us be contented with that state of life in which God has placed us; let our solicitude be not for earthly goods, but for those of Paradise, which are immeasurably greater, and last forever; and let us be fully persuaded of what St. Teresa says: "The less we have here, the more we shall have there."[15]

St. Bonaventure said that temporal goods were nothing more than a sort of birdlime to hinder the soul from flying to God. And St. John Climacus [16] said, that poverty, on the contrary, is a path which leads to God free of all hindrances. Our Lord himself said: Blessed are the poor in spirit, for theirs is the kingdom of heaven.[17] In the other Beatitudes, the heaven of the life to come is promised to the meek and to the clean of heart; but to the poor, heaven (that is, heavenly joy) is promised even in this life: theirs is the kingdom of heaven. Yes, for even in the present life the poor enjoy a foretaste of paradise. By the poor in spirit are meant those who are not merely poor in earthly goods, but who do not so much as desire them; who, having enough to clothe and feed them, live contented, according to the advice of the Apostle: But having food, and wherewith to be covered, with these we are content.[18] Oh, blessed poverty (exclaimed St. Laurence Justinian), which possesses nothing and fears nothing; she is ever joyous and ever in abundance, since she turns every inconvenience into advantage for the soul.[19] St. Bernard said: "The avaricious man hungers after earthly things as a beggar, the poor man despises them as a lord."[20] The miser is always hungry as a beggar, because he is never satiated with the possessions he desires; the poor man, on the contrary, despises them all as a rich lord, inasmuch as he desires nothing.

One day Jesus Christ thus spoke to the Blessed Angela of Foligno: "If poverty were not of great excellence, I would not have chosen it for myself, nor have bequeathed it to my elect." And, in fact, the saints, seeing Jesus poor, had therefore a great affection for poverty. St. Paul says, that the desire of growing rich is a snare of Satan, by which he has wrought the ruin of innumerable souls: They that will become rich, fall into temptation, and into the snare of the devil, and into many unprofitable and hurtful desires, which drown men into destruction and perdition.[21] Unhappy beings who, for the sake of vile creatures of earth, forfeit an infinite good, which is God! St. Basil the Martyr was quite in the right, when the Emperor Licinius proposed to make him the chief among his priests, if he would renounce Jesus Christ; he was right, I say, to reply: "Tell the emperor, that were he to give me his whole kingdom, he would not give me as much as he would rob me of, by depriving me of God."[22] Let us be content then with God, and with those things which he gives us, rejoicing in our poverty, when we stand in need of something we desire, and have it not; for herein consists our merit. "Not poverty," says St. Bernard, "but the love of poverty, is reckoned a virtue."[23] Many are poor, but from not loving their poverty, they merit nothing; therefore St. Bernard says, that the virtue of poverty consists not in being poor, but in the love of poverty.

This love of poverty should be especially practiced by religious who have made the vow of poverty. "Many religious," says the same St. Bernard, "wish to be poor; but on the condition of wanting for nothing."[24] "Thus," says St. Francis de Sales, "they wish for the honor of poverty, but not the inconveniences of poverty."[25] To such persons is applicable the saying of the Blessed Salomea, a nun of St. Clare: "That religious shall be a laughing-stock to angels and to men, who pretends to be poor, and yet murmurs when she is in want of something." Good religious act differently; they love their poverty above all riches. The daughter of the Emperor Maximilian II., a discalced nun of St. Clare, called Sister Margaret of the Cross, appeared on one occasion before her brother, the Archduke Albert, in a patched-up habit, who evinced some astonishment, as if it were unbecoming her noble birth; but she made him this answer: "My brother, I am more content with this torn garment than all monarchs with their purple robes." St. Mary Magdalene of Pazzi said: "O happy religious! who, detached from all by means of holy poverty, can say, The Lord is the portion of my inheritance.[26] "My God, Thou art my portion and all my good."[27] St. Teresa, having received a large alms from a certain merchant, sent him word that his name was written in the Book of Life, and that, in token of this, he should lose all his possessions; and the merchant actually failed, and remained in poverty till death. St. Aloysius Gonzaga said that there could be no surer sign that a person is numbered among the elect, than to see him fearing God, and at the same time undergoing crosses and tribulations in this life.

The bereavement of relatives and friends by death belongs also, in some measure, to holy poverty; and in this we must especially practice patience. Some people, at the loss of a parent or friend, can find no rest; they shut themselves up to weep in their chamber, and giving free vent to their sorrow, become insupportable to all around them, by their want of patience. I would ask these people, for whose gratification they thus lament and shed tears? For that of God? Certainly not, for God's will is, that they should be resigned to his dispensations. For that of the soul departed. By no means: if the soul be lost, she abhors both you and your tears; if she be saved, and already in heaven, she would have you thank God on her part; if still in purgatory, she craves the help of your prayers, and wishes you to bow with resignation to the divine will, and to become a saint, in order that she may one day enjoy your society in paradise. Of what use, then, is all this weeping? On one occasion, the Venerable Father Joseph Caracciolo, the Theatine, was surrounded by his relatives, who were all bitterly lamenting the death of his brother, whereupon he said to them: "Come, come! let us keep these tears for a better purpose, to weep over the death of Jesus Christ, who has been to us a father, a brother, and spouse, and who died for love of us." On such occasions we must imitate Job, who, on hearing the news of the death of his sons, exclaimed, with full resignation to the Divine will, The Lord gave, and the Lord hath taken away; God gave me my sons, and God hath taken them away. As it hath pleased the Lord, so is it done, blessed be the name of the Lord;[28] it hath pleased God that such things should happen, and so it pleases me; wherefore may he be blessed by me forever.

III.

Patience under Contempt.

In the third place, we must practice patience, and show our love to God, by tranquilly submitting to contempt.

As soon as a soul delivers herself up to God, he sends her from himself, or through others, insults, and persecution. One day an angel appeared to the Blessed Henry Suso and said to him, "Henry, thou hast hitherto mortified thyself in thy own way; henceforth thou shalt be mortified after the pleasure of others." On the day following, as he was looking from a window on the street, he saw a dog shaking and tearing a rag which it held in its mouth; at the same moment a voice said to him, "So hast thou to be torn in the mouths of men." Forthwith the Blessed Henry descended into the street and secured the rag, putting it by to encourage him in his coming trials.[29]

Affronts and injuries were the delicacies the saints earnestly longed and sought for. St. Philip Neri, during the space of thirty years, had to put up with much ill-treatment in the house of St. Jerome at Rome; but on this very account he refused to leave it, and resisted all the invitations of his sons to come and live with them in the new Oratory, founded by himself, till he received an express command from the Pope to do so. So St. John of the Cross was prescribed change of air for an illness which eventually carried him to the grave; now, he could have selected a more commodious convent, of which the Prior was particularly attached to him; but he chose instead a poor convent, whose Prior was his enemy, and who, in fact, for a long time, and almost up to his dying day, spoke ill of him, and abused him in many ways, and even prohibited the other monks from visiting him. Here we see how the saints even sought to be despised. St. Teresa wrote this admirable maxim: "Whoever aspires to perfection must beware of ever saying: They had no reason to treat me so. If you will not bear any cross but one which is founded on reason, then perfection is not for you." Whilst St. Peter Martyr was complaining in prison of being confined unjustly, he received that celebrated answer from the Crucifix: our Lord said to him, "And what evil have I done, that I suffer and die on this cross for men?" Oh, what consolation do the saints derive in all their tribulations from the ignominies which Jesus Christ endured! St. Eleazar, on being asked by his wife how he contrived to bear with so much patience the many injuries which he had to sustain, and that even from his own servants, replied: "I turn my looks on the outraged Jesus, and I discover immediately that my affronts are a mere nothing in comparison with what he suffered for my sake; and thus God gives me strength to support all patiently."

In fine, affronts, poverty, torments, and all tribulations, serve only to estrange further from God the soul that does not love him; whereas, when they befall a soul in love with God, they become an instrument of closer union and more ardent love of God: Many waters cannot quench charity.[30] However great and grievous troubles may be, so far from extinguishing the flames of charity, they only serve to enkindle them the more in a soul that loves nothing else but God.

But wherefore does Almighty God load us with so many crosses, and take pleasure in seeing us afflicted, reviled, persecuted, and ill-treated by the world? Is he, perchance, a tyrant, whose cruel disposition makes him rejoice in our suffering? No: God is by no means a tyrant, nor cruel; he is all compassion and love towards us; suffice it to say, that he has died for us. He indeed does rejoice at our suffering, but for our good; inasmuch as, by suffering here, we are released hereafter from the debt of torments justly due from us to his divine justice; he rejoices in them, because they detach us from the sensual pleasures of this world: when a mother would wean her child, she puts gall on the breast, in order to create a disgust in the child; he rejoices in them, because we give him, by our patience and resignation in bearing them, a token of our love; in fine, he rejoices in them, because they contribute to our increase of glory in heaven. Such are the reasons for which the Almighty, in his compassion and love towards us, is pleased at our suffering.

Let us now draw this chapter to a conclusion. That we may be able to practice patience to advantage in all our tribulations, we must be fully persuaded that every trial comes from the hands of God, either directly, or in directly through men; we must therefore render God thanks whenever we are beset with sorrows, and accept, with gladness of heart, of every event, prosperous or adverse, that proceeds from him, knowing that all happens by his disposition for our welfare: To them that love God all things work together unto good.[31] In addition to this, it is well in our tribulations to glance a moment at that hell which we have formerly deserved: for assuredly all the pains of this life are incomparably smaller than the awful pains of hell. But above all, prayer, by which we gain divine assistance, is the great means to suffer patiently all affliction, scorn, and contradictions; and is that which will furnish us with the strength which we have not of ourselves. The saints were persuaded of this; they recommended themselves to God, and so overcame every kind of torments and persecutions.

Affections and Prayers.

O Lord, I am fully persuaded that without suffering, and suffering with patience, I cannot win the crown of Paradise. David said: From Him is my patience.[32] And I say the same; my patience in suffering must come from Thee. I make many purposes to accept in peace of all tribulations; but no sooner are they at hand than I grow sad and alarmed; and if I suffer, I suffer without merit and without love, because I know not how to suffer them to please Thee. O my Jesus, through the merits of Thy patience in bearing so many afflictions for love of me, grant me the grace to bear crosses for the love of Thee! I love Thee with my whole heart, O my dear Redeemer! I love Thee, my sovereign good! I love Thee, my own love, worthy of infinite love. I am grieved at any displeasure I have ever caused Thee, more than for any evil whatever. I promise Thee to receive with patience all the trials Thou mayest send me; but I look to Thee for help to be faithful to my promise, and especially to be enabled to bear in peace the throes of my last agony and death.

Mary, my Queen, vouchsafe to obtain for me a true resignation in all the anguish and trials that await me in life and death.

CHARITY BELIEVETH ALL THINGS

HE THAT LOVES JESUS CHRIST BELIEVES ALL HIS WORDS

Whoever loves a person, believes all that proceeds from the lips of that person; consequently, the more a soul loves Jesus Christ, the livelier and more unshaken is her faith. When the good thief beheld our Redeemer, though he had done no ill, suffering death upon the cross with such patience, he began at once to love him; under the influence of this love, and of the divine light which then broke upon his soul, he believed that this was truly the Son of God, and begged not to be forgotten by him when he should have passed into his kingdom.

Faith is the foundation of charity; but faith afterwards receives its perfection from charity. His faith is most perfect whose love of God is most perfect. Charity produces in man not merely the faith of the understanding, but the faith of the will also: those who believe only with the understanding, but not with the will, as is the case with sinners who are perfectly convinced of the truths of the faith, but do not choose to live according to the divine commandments,—such as these have a very weak faith; for had they a more lively belief that the grace of God is a priceless treasure, and that sin, because it. robs us of this grace, is the worst of evils, they would assuredly change their lives. If, then, they prefer the miserable creatures of this earth to God, it is because they either do not believe, or because their faith is very weak. On the contrary, he who believes not only with the understanding, but also with the will, so that he not only believes, but has the will to believe in God, the revealer of truth, from the love he has for him, and rejoices in so believing,—such a one has a perfect faith, and consequently seeks to make his life conformable to the truths that he believes.

Weakness of faith, however, in those who live in sin, does not spring from the obscurity of faith; for though God, in order to make our faith more meritorious, has veiled the objects of faith in darkness and secrecy, he has at the same time given us so clear and convincing evidence of their truth, that not to believe them would argue not merely a lack of sense, but sheer madness and impiety. The weakness of the faith of many people is to be traced to their wickedness of living. He who, rather than forego the enjoyment of forbidden pleasures, scorns the divine friendship, would wish there were no law to forbid, and no chastisement to punish, his sin; on this account he strives to blind himself to the eternal truths of death, judgment, and hell, and of divine justice; and because such subjects strike too much terror into his heart, and are too apt to mix bitterness in his cup of pleasure, he sets his brain to work to discover proofs, which have at least the look of plausibility; and by which he allows himself to be flattered into the persuasion that there is no soul, no God, no hell, in order that he may live and die like the brute beasts, without laws and without reason.

And this laxity of morals is the source whence have issued, and still issue daily, so many books and systems of Materialists, Indifferentists, Politicists, Deists, and Naturalists; some among them deny the divine existence, and some the divine Providence, saying that God, after having created men, takes no further notice of them, and is heedless whether they love or hate him whether they be saved or lost; others, again, deny the goodness of God, and maintain that he has created numberless souls for hell, becoming himself their tempter to sin, that so they may damn themselves, and go into everlasting fire, to curse him there forever.

Oh, ingratitude and wickedness of men! God has created them in his mercy, to make them eternally happy in heaven; he has poured on them so many lights, benefits, and graces, to bring them to eternal life; for the same end he has redeemed them at the price of so many sorrows and sufferings; and yet they strive to deny all, that they may give free rein to their vicious inclinations! But no: let them strive as they will, the unhappy beings cannot wrest themselves from remorse of conscience, and the dread of divine vengeance. On this subject I have latterly published a work, entitled The Truth of Faith, in which I have clearly shown the inconsistency of all these systems of modern unbelievers. Oh, if they would but once forsake sin, and apply themselves earnestly to the love of Jesus Christ, they would then most certainly cast away all doubts about things of faith, and firmly believe all the truths that God has revealed!

The true lover of Jesus Christ keeps the eternal truths constantly in view and orders all his actions according to them. Oh, how thoroughly does he who loves Jesus Christ understand the force of that saying of the Wise Man, Vanity of vanities, and all is vanity.[1] that all earthly greatness is mere smoke, dirt, and delusion; that the soul's only welfare and happiness consists in loving its Creator, and in doing his blessed will; that we are, in reality, no more than what we are before God; that it is of no use to gain the whole world, if the soul be lost; that all the goods in the world can never satisfy the hu man heart, but only God himself; and, in fine, that we must leave all in order to gain all.

Charity believeth all things.[2] There are other Christians, though not so perverse as the class we have mentioned, who would fain believe in nothing, that they may give full scope to their unruly passions, and live on undisturbed by the stings of remorse, there are others, I say, who believe, indeed, but their faith is languid; they believe the most holy mysteries of religion, the truths of Revelation contained in the Gospel, the Trinity, the Redemption, the holy Sacraments, and the rest; still they do not believe all. Jesus Christ has said: Blessed are the poor; blessed are the sorrowful; blessed are the mortified; blessed are those whom men persecute, calumniate, and curse. Blessed are the poor; blessed are they that hunger; blessed are they that suffer persecution; blessed are you when men shall revile you and shall say all manner of evil against you.[3] This is the teaching of Jesus Christ in the Gospel. How, then, can it be said, that those believe in the Gospel who say: "Blessed are those who have money; blessed are those who suffer nothing; blessed are those who can take their amusements; pitiable is the man that suffers persecution and ill-treatment from others"? We must certainly say of such as these, that either they do not believe the Gospel, or that they believe only a part of it. He who believes it all esteems it his highest fortune, and a mark of the divine favor in this world, to be poor, to be sick, to be mortified, to be despised and ill-treated by men. Such is the belief, and such the language, of one who believes all that is said in the Gospel and has a real love for Jesus Christ.

Affections and Prayers.

My beloved Redeemer, O life of my soul, I firmly believe that Thou art the only good worthy of being loved. I believe that Thou art the greatest lover of my soul, since through love alone Thou didst die, overwhelmed with sorrows for love of me. I believe there is no greater blessing in this world, or in the next, than to love Thee, and to do Thy adorable will. All this I believe most firmly; so that I renounce all things, that I may belong wholly to Thee, and that I may possess Thee alone. Help me, through the merits of Thy sacred Passion, and make me such as Thou wouldst have me to be. I believe in Thee, O infallible truth! I trust in Thee, O infinite mercy! I love Thee, O infinite goodness! O infinite love, I give myself wholly to Thee, who hast wholly given Thyself to me in Thy Passion, and in the holy Sacrament of the Altar. And I recommend myself to Thee, O Mary, refuge of sinners, and Mother of God!

CHARITY HOPETH ALL THINGS

HE THAT LOVES JESUS CHRIST HOPES FOR ALL THINGS FROM HIM

Hope increases charity, and charity increases hope. Hope in the Divine goodness undoubtedly gives an increase to our love of Jesus Christ. St. Thomas says, that in the very
moment when we hope to receive some benefit from a person, we begin also to love him.
[1] On this account, the Lord forbids us to put our trust in creatures: Put not your trust in
princes. [2] Further, He pronounces a curse on those who do so: Cursed be the man that
trusted in man. [3] God does not wish us to trust in creatures, because He does not wish
us to fix our love upon them. Hence St. Vincent of Paul said: "Let us beware of reposing
too much confidence in men; for when God beholds us thus leaning on them for support,
He Himself withdraws from us." On the other hand, the more we trust in God, the more
we shall advance in His holy love: I have run the way of Thy Commandments, when Thou
didst enlarge my heart. [4] Oh, how rapidly does that soul advance in perfection that has
her heart dilated with confidence in God! She flies rather than runs; for by making God the
foundation of all her hope, she flings aside her own weakness, and borrows the strength
of God Himself, which is communicated to all who place their confidence in Him: They
that hope in the Lord shall renew their strength, they shall take wings as eagles, they shall
run and not be weary, they shall walk and not faint. [5] The eagle is the bird that soars
nearest the sun; in like manner, the soul that has God for her trust becomes detached
from the earth, and more and more united to God by love.

Now as hope increases the love of God, so does love help to increase hope; for charity makes us the adopted sons of God. In the natural order we are the work of His hands; but in the supernatural order we are made sons of God, and partakers of the Divine nature, through the merits of Jesus Christ; as the Apostle St. Peter writes: That by these you may be made partakers of the Divine nature. [6] And if charity makes us the sons of God, it consequently makes us heirs of Heaven, according to St. Paul: And if sons, heirs also. [7] Now a son claims the right of abiding under the paternal roof; an heir is entitled to the property; and thus, charity increases the hope of Paradise: so that the souls that love God cry out incessantly, "Thy kingdom come, Thy kingdom come!" Moreover, God loves those who love Him: I love them that love Me. [8] He showers down His graces on those that seek Him by love: The Lord is good to the soul that seeks Him. [9] Consequently, the soul that loves God most has the greatest hope in His goodness. This confidence produces that imperturbable tranquility in the Saints which makes them always joyful and full of peace, even amid the severest trials; for their love of Jesus Christ, and their persuasion of His liberality towards those who love Him, leads them to trust solely in Him; and thus, they find a lasting repose. The sacred spouse abounded with delights, because she loved none but her Spouse, and leaned entirely on Him for support; she was full of contentment, since she well knew how generous her beloved is towards all that love Him; so that of her it is written: Who is this that cometh up from the desert, flowing with delights, leaning upon her Beloved? [10] These words of the Wise Man are most true: All good things come to me together with her. [11] With charity, all blessings are introduced into the soul.

The primary object of Christian hope is God, Whom the soul enjoys in the kingdom of Heaven. But we must not suppose that the hope of enjoying God in Paradise is any obstacle to charity; since the hope of Paradise is inseparably connected with charity, which there receives its full and complete perfection. Charity is that infinite treasure, spoken of by the Wise Man, which makes us the friends of God: An infinite treasure to men, which they that use become the friends of God. [12] The angelic Doctor St. Thomas says that friendship is founded on the mutual communication of goods; for as friendship is nothing more than a mutual love between friends, it follows that there must be a reciprocal interchange of the good which each possesses. [13] Hence the Saint says: "If there be no communication, there is no friendship." On this account Jesus Christ says to His disciples: I have called you friends, because all things whatsoever I have heard of My Father I have made known to you. [14] Since He had made them His friends, He had communicated all His secrets to them. St. Francis de Sales says: "If, by a supposition of what is impossible, there could be an infinite good (that is a God) to Whom we belonged in no way whatever, and with Whom we could have no union or communication, we should certainly esteem Him more than ourselves; so that we might feel great desire of being able to love Him; but we should not actually love Him, because love is built upon union; for love is a friendship, and the foundation of friendship is to have things in common; and its end is union." [15.] Thus St. Thomas teaches us that charity does not exclude the desire of the reward prepared for us in Heaven by Almighty God. On the contrary, it makes us look to it as the chief object of our love, for such is God, Who constitutes the bliss of Paradise; for friendship implies, that friends rejoice with one another.

The Spouse in the Canticles refers to this reciprocal interchange of goods when she says: My Beloved to me and I to Him. [16] In Heaven the soul belongs wholly to God, and God belongs wholly to the soul, according to the measure of her capacity and of her merits. But from the persuasion which the soul has of her own nothingness in comparison with the infinite attractions of Almighty God, and aware consequently that the claims of God on her love are beyond measure greater than her own can be on the love of God, she is therefore more anxious to procure the Divine pleasure than her own enjoyment; so that she is more gratified by the pleasure which she affords Almighty God by giving herself entirely to Him, than by God's giving Himself entirely to her; but at the same time she is delighted when God thus gives Himself to her, inasmuch as she is thereby animated to give herself up to God with a greater intensity of love. Site indeed rejoices at the glory which God imparts to her, but for the sole purpose of referring it back to God Himself, and of thus doing her utmost to increase the Divine glory. At the sight of God in Heaven the soul cannot help loving Him with all her strength; on the other hand, God cannot hate anyone that loves Him: but if (supposing what is impossible) God could hate a soul that loves Him, and if a beatified soul could exist without loving God, she would much rather endure all the pains of Hell, on condition of being allowed to love God as much as He should hate her, than to live without loving God, even though she could enjoy all the other delights of Paradise. So it is; for that conviction which the soul has of God's boundless claims upon her love gives her a greater desire to love God than to be loved by Him.

St. Thomas, with the Master of the Sentences, defines Christian hope to be a "sure expectation of eternal happiness." [17] Its certainty arises from the infallible promise of

God to give eternal life to His faithful servants. Now charity, by taking away sin, at the same time takes away all obstacles to our obtaining the happiness of the blessed; hence the greater our charity, the greater also and firmer is our hope. Hope, on the other hand, can in no way interfere with the purity of love, because, according to the observation of St. Dionysius the Areopagite, love tends naturally to union with the object beloved; or, as St. Augustine asserts in stronger terms, love itself is like a chain of gold that links together the hearts of the lover and the loved. "Love is as it were a kind of bond uniting two together." [18] And as this union can never be affected at a distance, the person that loves always longs for the presence of the object of his love. The sacred spouse languished in the absence of her beloved. and entreated her companions to acquaint Him with her sorrow, that He might come and console her with His Presence: I adjure you, O daughters of Jerusalem, if you find my Beloved, that you tell Him that I languish with love. [19] A soul that loves Jesus Christ exceedingly cannot but desire and hope, if she remains on earth, to go without delay and be united to her beloved Lord in Heaven.

Thus, we see that the desire to go and see God in Heaven, not so much for the delight which we shall experience in loving God, as for the pleasure which we shall afford God by loving Him, is pure and perfect love. Nor is the joy of the blessed in Heaven any hindrance to the purity of their love; such joy is inseparable from their love; but they take far more satisfaction in their love of God than in the joy that it affords them. Someone will perhaps say: But the desire for a reward is rather a love of concupiscence than a love of friendship. We must therefore make a distinction between temporal rewards promised by men and the eternal rewards of Paradise promised by God to those who love Him: the rewards given by man are distinct from their own persons and independent of them, since they do not bestow themselves, but only their goods, when they would remunerate others; on the contrary, the principal reward which God gives to the blessed is the gift of Himself: I am thy reward exceeding great. [20] Hence to desire Heaven is the same thing as to desire God, Who is our last end.

I wish here to propose a doubt, which may rise in the mind of one who loves God and strives to conform himself in all things to His blessed will. If it should be ever revealed to such a one that he would be eternally lost, would he be obliged to bow to it with resignation, to practice conformity with the will of God? St. Thomas says no; and further, that he would sin by consenting to it, because he would be consenting to live in a state that involves sin, and is contrary to the last end for which God created him; for God did not create souls to hate Him in Hell, but to love Him in Heaven: so that He does not wish the death even of the sinner, but that all should be converted and saved. The holy Doctor says that God wishes no one to be damned except through sin; and therefore, a person, by consenting to his damnation, would not be acting in conformity with the will of God, but with the will of sin. [21] But suppose that God, foreseeing the sin of a person, should have decreed his damnation, and that this decree should be revealed to him, would he be bound to consent to it? In the same passage the Saint says, by no means; because such a revelation must not be taken as an irrevocable decree, but made merely by way of communication, as a threat of what would follow if he persisted in sin.

But let everyone banish such baneful thoughts from his mind, as only calculated to cool his confidence and love. Let us love Jesus Christ as much as possible here below; let us always be sighing to go hence and to behold Him in Paradise, that we may there love Him perfectly; let us make it the grand object of all our hopes, to go thither to love Him with all our strength. We are commanded even in this life to love God with our whole strength: Thou shalt love the Lord thy God with thy whole heart, with thy whole soul, and with all thy strength; [22] but the angelic Doctor [23] says that man cannot perfectly fulfill this precept upon earth; only Jesus Christ, Who was both God and Man, and the most holy Mary, who was full of grace and free from Original Sin, perfectly fulfilled it. But we miserable children of Adam, infected as we are with sin, cannot love God without some imperfection; and it is in Heaven alone, when we shall see God face to face, that we shall love Him, nay more, that we shall be necessitated to love Him with all our strength.

Behold, then, the scope of all our desires and aspirations, of all our thoughts and ardent hopes; to go and enjoy God in Heaven, to love Him with all our strength, and to rejoice in the enjoyment of God. The blessed certainly rejoice in their own felicity in that kingdom of delights; but the chief source of their happiness, and that which absorbs all the rest, is to know that their beloved Lord possesses an infinite happiness; for they love God incomparably more than themselves. Each one of the blessed has such a love for Him, that he would willingly forfeit all happiness, and undergo the cruelest torments, rather than that God should lose (if it were possible for Him to lose) one, even the least particle of His happiness. Hence the sight of God's infinite happiness, and the knowledge that it can never suffer diminution for all eternity, constitutes his Paradise. This is the meaning of what our Lord says to every soul on whom He bestows the possession of eternal glory: Enter the joy of thy Lord. [24] It is not the joy that enters the blessed soul, but the soul that enters the joy of God, since the joy of God is the object of the joy of the blessed. Thus, the good of God will be the good of the blessed; the riches of God will be their riches, and the happiness of God will be their happiness.

On the instant that a soul enters Heaven and sees by the light of glory the infinite beauty of God face to face, she is at once seized and all consumed with love. The happy soul is then as it were lost and immersed in that boundless ocean of the goodness of God. Then it is that she quite forgets herself, and inebriated with Divine love, thinks only of loving her God: They shall be inebriated with the plenty of Thy House. [25] As an intoxicated person no longer thinks of himself, so a soul in bliss can only think of loving and affording delight to her beloved Lord; she desires to possess Him entirely, and she does in fact possess Him, without fear of losing Him anymore; she desires to give herself wholly to Him, at every moment, and she does indeed possess Him for every moment she offers herself to God without reserve, and God receives her in His loving embraces, and so holds her, and shall hold her in the same fond embraces for all eternity.

In this manner the soul is wholly united to God in Heaven and loves Him with all her strength; her love is most perfect and complete, and though necessarily finite, since a creature is not capable of infinite love, it nevertheless renders her perfectly happy and contented, so that she desires nothing more. On the other hand, Almighty God communicates Himself, and unites Himself wholly to the soul, filling her with Himself proportionately to her merits; and this union is not merely by means only of His gifts, lights, and loving attractions, as is the case during the present life, but by His Own very essence. As fire penetrates iron, and seems to change it into itself, so does God penetrate the soul and fill her with Himself; and though she never loses her own being, yet she becomes so penetrated and absorbed by that immense ocean of the Divine substance, that she remains, as it were, annihilated, and as if she ceased to exist. The Apostle prayed for this happy lot for His disciples when He said: That you may be filled unto all the fullness of God. [26]

And this is the last end, which the goodness of God has appointed for us in the life to come. Hence the soul can never enjoy perfect repose on earth; because it is only in Heaven that she can obtain perfect union with God. It is true that the lovers of Jesus Christ find peace in the practice of perfect conformity with the will of God; but they cannot in this life find complete repose; this is only obtained when our last end is obtained; that is, when we see God face to face, and are consumed with His Divine love; and as long as the soul does not reach this end, she is ill at ease, and groans and sighs, saying: Behold, in peace is my bitterness most bitter. [27] Yes, O my God, I live in peace in this valley of tears, because such is Thy will; but I cannot help feeling unspeakable bitterness at finding myself at a distance from Thee, and not yet perfectly united with Thee, Who art my center my all, and the fullness of my repose!

For this reason, the Saints, though they were all inflamed with the love of God, did nothing but sigh after Paradise. David cried out: Woe is me, that my sojourning is prolonged! [28] I shall be satisfied when thy glory shall appear. [29] St. Paul said of himself: Having a desire to be with Christ. [30] St. Francis of Assisi said:

> "I look for such a need of bliss,
> That all my pain seems happiness." [31]

These were all so many acts of perfect charity, The angelic Doctor teaches us, that the highest degree of charity that a soul can reach upon earth, is to desire intensely to go and be united with God, and to enjoy Him in Heaven. [32] But, as we have already seen, this enjoyment of God in Heaven does not consist so much in the fruition of the delights there lavished on her by Almighty God, as in the pleasure she takes in the happiness of God Himself, Whom she loves incomparably more than herself.

The Holy Souls in Purgatory feel no pain more acutely than that of their yearning to possess God, from Whom they remain still at a distance. And this sort of pain will afflict those especially who in their lifetime had but little desire of Paradise. Cardinal Bellarmine [33] also says, that there is a certain place in Purgatory called, 'prison of honor,' where certain souls are not tormented with any pain of sense, but merely with the pain of privation of the sight of God; examples of this are related by St. Gregory, Venerable Bede, St. Vincent Ferrer, and St. Bridget; and this punishment is not for the commission of sin, but for coldness in desiring Heaven. Many souls aspire to perfection; but for the rest, they are too indifferent whether they go to enjoy the sight of God or continue on earth. But eternal life is an inestimable good, that has been purchased by the death of Jesus Christ; and God punishes such souls as have been remiss during life in their desires to obtain it.

Affections and Prayers

O God, my Creator and my Redeemer, Thou hast created me for Heaven; Thou hast redeemed me from Hell to bring me into Heaven; and I have so many times, in Thy very face, renounced my claim to Heaven by my sins, and have remained contented in seeing myself doomed to Hell! But blessed forever be Thy infinite mercy, which, I hope, has pardoned me, and many a time rescued me from perdition. Ah, my Jesus, would that I had never offended Thee! would that I had always loved Thee! I am glad that at least I still have time to do so. I love Thee! O love of my soul, I love Thee with my whole heart; I love Thee more than myself! I see plainly that Thou wish to save me, that I may be able to love Thee for all eternity in that kingdom of love. I thank Thee and beseech Thee to help me for the remainder of my life, in which I wish to love Thee most ardently, that I may ardently love Thee in eternity. Ah, my Jesus. When will the day arrive that shall free me from all danger of losing Thee, that shall consume me with love, by unveiling before my eyes Thine infinite beauty, so that I shall be under the necessity of loving Thee? Oh, sweet necessity! Oh, happy and dear and most desired necessity, which shall relieve me from all fear of ever more displeasing Thee and shall oblige me to love Thee with all my strength! My conscience alarms me, and says: "How canst Thou presume to enter Heaven?" But, my dearest Redeemer, Thy merits are all my hope.

O Mary, Queen of Heaven, thy intercession is all-powerful with God, in thee I put my trust!

CHARITY BEARETH ALL THINGS

HE THAT LOVES JESUS CHRIST WITH A STRONG LOVE DOES NOT CEASE TO LOVE HIM IN THE MIDST OF ALL SORTS OF TEMPTATIONS AND DESOLATIONS

It is not the pains of poverty, of sickness, of dishonor and persecution, which in this life most afflict the souls that love God, but temptations and desolations of spirit. Whilst a soul is in the enjoyment of the loving presence of God, she is so far from grieving at all the afflictions and ignominies and outrages of men, that, she is rather comforted by them, as they afford her an opportunity of showing God a token of her love; they serve, in short, as fuel to enkindle her love more and more. But to find herself solicited by temptations to forfeit the Divine grace, or in the hour of desolation to apprehend having already lost it, oh, these are torments too cruel to bear for one who loves Jesus Christ with all her heart! However, the same love supplies her with strength to endure all patiently, and to pursue the way of perfection, on which she has entered. And, oh, what progress do those souls make by means of these trials, which God is pleased to send them to prove their love!

I.

Temptations.

Temptations are the most grievous trials that can happen to a soul that loves Jesus Christ; she accepts with resignation of every other evil, as calculated only to bind her in closer union with God; but temptations to commit sin would drive her, as we said above, to a separation from Jesus Christ; and on this account they are more intolerable to her than all other afflictions.

Why God permits Temptations

We must know, however, that although no temptation to evil can ever come from God, but only from the devil or our own corrupt inclinations: for God is not a tempter of evils, and he tempted no man; [1] nevertheless, God does at times permit His most cherished souls to be the most grievously tempted.

In the first place, in order that from temptations the soul may better learn her own weakness, and the need she has of the Divine assistance not to fall. Whilst a soul is favored with heavenly consolations, she feels as if she were able to vanquish every assault of the enemy, and to achieve every undertaking for the glory of God. But when she is strongly tempted and is almost reeling on the edge of the precipice, and just ready to fall, then she becomes better acquainted with her own misery and with her inability to resist, if God did not come to her rescue. So, it fared with St. Paul, who tells us that God had suffered him to be troubled with a temptation to sensual pleasure, to keep him humble after the revelations with which God had favored him: And lest the greatness of the revelations should exalt me, there was given me a sting of my flesh, an Angel of Satan to buffet me. [2]

Besides, God permits temptations with a view to detach us more thoroughly from this life; and to kindle in us the desire to go and behold Him in Heaven. Hence pious souls, finding themselves attacked day and night by so many enemies, come at length to feel a loathing for life, and exclaim: Woe is me, that my sojourning is prolonged! [3] And they sigh for the moment when they can say: The snare is broken, and we are delivered. [4] The soul would willingly wing her flight to God; but as long as she lives upon this earth, she is bound by a snare which detains her here below, where she is continually assailed with temptations; this snare is only broken by death: so that the souls that love God sigh for death, which will deliver them from all danger of losing Him.

Almighty God, moreover, allows us to be tempted, to make us richer in merits, as it was said to Tobias: And because thou was acceptable to God, it was necessary that temptations should prove thee. [5] Thus, a soul need not imagine herself out of God's favor because she is tempted but should make it rather a motive of hope that God loves her. It is a delusion of the devil to lead some pusillanimous people to suppose that temptations are sins that contaminate the soul. It is not bad thoughts that make us lose God, but the consenting to them; let the suggestions of the devil be ever so violent, let those filthy imaginations which overload our minds be ever so lively, they cannot cast the least stain on our souls, provided only we yield no consent to them; on the contrary, they make the soul purer, stronger, and dearer to Almighty God. St. Bernard says that every time we overcome a temptation, we win a fresh crown in Heaven: "As often as we conquer, so often are we crowned." [6] An Angel once appeared to a Cistercian monk, and put a crown into his hands, with orders that he should carry it to one of his fellow-religious, as a reward for the temptation that he had lately overcome.

Nor must we be disturbed if evil thoughts do not forthwith disappear from our minds but continue obstinately to persecute us; it is enough if we detest them and do our best to banish them. God is faithful, says the Apostle; He will not allow us to be tempted above our strength: God is faithful, Who will not suffer you to be tempted above that which you are able; but will make also with temptation issue, that you may be able to bear it. [7] Thus, a person, so far from losing anything by temptations, derives great profit from them. On this account God frequently allows the souls dearest to Him to undergo the severest temptations, that they may turn them into a source of greater merit on earth, and of greater glory in Heaven. Stagnant water soon grows putrid; a soul left at ease, without any struggle or temptation, stands in great danger of perishing from some self-conceit of her own merit; she perhaps imagines herself to have already attained to perfection, and therefore has little fear; and consequently takes little pains to recommend herself to God and to secure her salvation; but when, on the contrary, she is agitated by temptations, and sees herself in danger of rushing headlong into sin, then she has recourse to God; she goes to the divine Mother; she renews her resolution rather to die than to sin; she humbles herself, and casts herself into the arms of the Divine mercy: in this manner, as experience shows us, the soul acquires fresh strength and closer union with God.

This must not, however, lead us to seek after temptations; on the contrary, we must pray to God to deliver us from temptations, and from those more especially by which God foresees we should be overcome; and this is precisely the object of that petition of the Our Father: Lead us not into temptation; [8] but when, by God's permission, we are beset with temptations, we must then, without either being alarmed or discouraged by those foul thoughts, rely wholly on Jesus Christ, and beseech Him to help us; and He, on His part, will not fail to give us the strength to resist. St. Augustine says: "Throw thyself on Him, and fear not; He will not withdraw to let thee fall." [9]

Remedies against Temptations

Let us come now to the means which we must employ to vanquish temptations. Spiritual masters prescribe a variety of means; but the most necessary, and the safest (of which only I will here speak), is to have immediate recourse to God with all humility and confidence; saying: Incline unto my aid, O God, O Lord, make haste to help me! [10] This short prayer will enable us to overcome the assaults of all the devils of Hell; for God is infinitely more powerful than all of them. Almighty God knows well that of ourselves we are unable to resist the temptations of the infernal powers; and on this account the most learned Cardinal Gotti remarks, "that whenever we are assailed, and in danger of being overcome, God is obliged to give us strength enough to resist as often as we call upon Him for it." [11]

And how can we doubt of receiving help from Jesus Christ, after all the promises that He has made us in the Holy Scriptures? Come to Me, all you that labor and are heavy laden, and I will refresh you. [12] Come to me, ye who are wearied in fighting against temptations, and I will restore your strength. Call upon Me in the day of trouble; I will deliver thee, and thou shalt honor Me. [13] When thou see thyself troubled by thine enemies, call upon Me, and I will bring thee out of the danger, and thou shalt praise Me. Then shalt thou call, and the Lord shall hear; thou shalt cry, and He shall say, Here I am. [14] Then shalt thou call upon the Lord for help, and He will hear thee: thou shalt cry out, Quick, O Lord, help me! and He will say to thee, Behold, here I am, I am present to help thee. Who hath called upon Him, and He despised him? [15] And who, says the prophet, has ever called upon God, and God has despised him without giving him help? David felt sure of never falling prey to his enemies, whilst he could have recourse to prayer; he says; Praising, I will call upon the Lord; and I shall be saved from my enemies. [16] For he well knew that God is close to all who invoke His aid: The Lord is nigh unto all of them that call upon Him. [17] And St. Paul adds that the Lord is by no means sparing but lavish of graces towards all that pray to Him: Rich unto all that call upon Him. [18]

Oh, would to God that all men would have recourse to Him whenever they are tempted to offend Him; they would then certainly never commit sin! They unhappily fall, because, led away by the cravings of their vicious appetites, they prefer to lose God, the sovereign good, then to forego their wretched short-lived pleasures. Experience gives us manifest proofs that whoever calls on God in temptation does not fall; and whoever fails to call on Him as surely falls and this is especially true of temptations to impurity. Solomon himself said that he knew very well he could not be chaste, unless God gave him the grace to be so; and he therefore invoked Him by prayer in the moment of temptation: And as I knew that I could not otherwise be continent, except God give it, . . . I went to the Lord and besought Him. [19] In temptations against purity (and the same holds good with regard to those against faith), we must take it as a rule never to strive to combat the temptation hand to hand; but we must endeavor immediately to get rid of it indirectly by making a good act of the love of God or of sorrow for our sins, or else by applying ourselves to some indifferent occupation calculated to distract us. At the very instant that we discover a thought of evil tendency, we must disown it immediately, and (so to speak) close the door in its face, and deny it all entrance into the mind, without tarrying in the least to examine its object or errand. We must cast away these foul suggestions as quickly as we could shake off a hot spark from the fire.

If the impure temptation has already forced its way into the mind, and plainly pictures its object to the imagination, to stir the passions, then, according to the advice of St. Jerome, we must burst forth into these words: "O Lord, Thou art my helper." [20] As soon, says the Saint, as we feel the sting of concupiscence, we must have recourse to God, and say: "O Lord, do Thou assist me;" we must invoke the most holy names of Jesus and Mary, which possess a wonderful efficacy in the suppression of temptations of this nature. St. Francis de Sales says, that no sooner do children espy a wolf than they instantly seek refuge in the arms of their father and mother; and there they remain out of all danger. Our conduct must be the same: we must flee without delay for succor to Jesus and Mary, by earnestly calling upon them. I repeat that we must instantly have recourse to them, without giving a moment's audience to the temptation, or disputing it. It is related in the fourth paragraph of the Book of Sentences of the Fathers, [21] that one day St. Pacomius heard the devil boasting that he had frequently got the better of a certain monk on account of his lending ear to him, and not turning instantly to call upon God. He heard another devil, on the contrary, utter this complaint: As for me, I can do nothing with my monk, because he never fails to have recourse to God, and always defeats me.

Should temptation, however, obstinately persist in attacking us, let us beware of becoming troubled or angry at it; for this might put it in the power of our enemy to overcome us. We must, on such occasions, make an act of humble resignation to the will of God, Who thinks fit to allow us to be tormented by these abominable temptations; and we must say: O Lord, I deserve to be molested with these filthy suggestions, in punishment of my past sins; but Thou must help to free me. And if the temptation lasts, let us never cease calling on Jesus and Mary. It is also very profitable, in the like importunity of temptations, to renew our firm purpose to God of suffering every torment, and a thousand deaths, rather than offend Him; and at the same time, we must invoke His Divine assistance. And even should the temptation be of such violence as to put us in imminent risk of consenting to it, we must then redouble our prayers, hasten into the presence of the Blessed Sacrament, cast ourselves at the feet of the Crucifix, or of some image of our Blessed Lady, and there pray with increased fervor, and cry out for help with groans and tears. God is certainly ready to hear all who pray to Him; and it is from Him alone, and not from our own exertions, that we must look for strength to resist; but sometimes Almighty God wills these struggles of us, and then He makes up for our weakness, and grants us the victory. It is also an excellent practice, in the moment of temptation, to make the Sign of the Cross on the forehead and breast. It is also of great service to discover the temptation to our spiritual director. St. Philip Neri used to say, that a temptation disclosed is half overcome.

Here it will be well to remark, what is unanimously admitted by all theologians, even of the rigorist school, that persons who have during a considerable period of time been leading a virtuous life, and live habitually in the fear of God, whenever they are in doubt, and are not certain whether they have given consent to a grievous sin, ought to be perfectly assured that they have not lost the Divine grace; for it is morally impossible that the will, confirmed in its good purposes for a considerable lapse of time, should on a sudden undergo so total a change as at once to consent to a mortal sin without clearly knowing it; the reason of it is, that mortal sin is so horrible a monster that it cannot possible enter a soul by which it has long been held in abhorrence, without her being fully aware of it. We have proved this at length in our Moral Theology. [22] St. Teresa said: No one is lost without knowing it; and no one is deceived without the will to be deceived. [23]

Wherefore, with regard to certain souls of delicate conscience, and solidly rooted in virtue, but at the same time timid and molested with temptations (especially if they be against faith or chastity), the director will find it sometimes expedient to forbid them to discover them or make any mention of them; because, if they have to mention them they are led to consider how such thoughts got entrance into their minds, and whether they paused to dispute with them, or took any complacency in them, or gave any consent to them; and so, by this too great reflection, those evil imaginations make a still deeper impression on their minds, and disturb them the more. Whenever the confessor is morally certain that the penitent has not consented to these suggestions, the best way is to forbid him to speak any more about them. And I find that St. Jane Frances de Chantal acted precisely in this manner. She relates of herself, that she was for several years assailed by the most violent storms of temptation, but had never spoken of them in Confession, since she was not conscious of having ever yielded to them; and in this she had only followed faithfully the rule received from her director. She says, "I never had a full conviction of having consented." [24] These words give us to understand that the temptations did produce in her some agitation from scruples; but despite these, she resumed her tranquility on the strength of the obedience imposed by her confessor, not to confess similar doubts. With this exception, it will be generally found an admirable means of quelling the violence of temptations to lay them open to our director, as we have said above.

But I repeat, the most efficacious and the most necessary of all remedies against temptations, is that remedy of all remedies, namely, to pray to God for help, and to continue praying as long as the temptation continues. Almighty God will frequently have decreed success, not to the first prayer, but to the second, third, or fourth. In short, we must be thoroughly persuaded that all our welfare depends on prayer: our amendment of life depends on prayer; our victory over temptations depends on prayer; on prayer depends on our obtaining Divine love, together with perfection, perseverance, and eternal salvation.

There may be some who, after the perusal of my spiritual works, will accuse me of tediousness in so often recommending the importance and necessity of having continual recourse to God by prayer. But I seem to myself to have said not too much, but far too little. I know that day and night we are all assailed with temptations from the infernal powers, and that Satan lets slip no occasion of causing us to fall. I know that, without the Divine help, we have not strength to repel the assaults of the devils; and that therefore the Apostle exhorts us to put on the armor of God: Put you on the armor of God, that you may be able to stand against the deceit of the devil. For our wrestling is not against flesh and blood, but against principalities and powers, against the rulers of the world of this darkness. [25] And what is this armor with which St. Paul warns us to clothe ourselves to conquer our enemies? Behold of what it consists of: By all prayer and supplication, always praying in the spirit, and in the same watching with all instances. [26] This armor is constant and fervent prayer to God, that He may help us to gain the victory. I know, moreover, that in every page of the Holy Scriptures, both in the Old and the New Testament, we are repeatedly admonished to pray: Call upon Me, and I will deliver thee. [27] Cry to Me, and I will hear thee. [28] We ought always to pray, and not to faint. [29] Ask, and you shall receive. [30] Watch and pray. [31] Pray without ceasing. [32] So that I think, far from having spoken too much on prayer, I have not said enough. I would urge it on all preachers, to recommend nothing so much to their audience as prayer; on confessors, to insist on nothing so earnestly with their penitents as prayer; on spiritual writers, to treat on no subject more copiously than on prayer. But it is a source of grief to my heart, and it seems to me a chastisement of our sins, that so many preachers, confessors, and authors speak so little of prayer. There is no doubt that sermons, meditations, Communions, and mortifications are great helps in the spiritual life; but if we fail to call upon God by prayer in the moment of temptation, we shall fall, despite all the sermons, meditations, Communions, penances, and virtuous resolutions. If then, we really wish to be saved, let us always pray, and commend ourselves to Jesus Christ, and most of all when we are tempted; and let us not only pray for the grace of holy perseverance, but at the same time for the grace to pray always. Let us, likewise, take care to recommend ourselves to the divine Mother, who, as St. Bernard says, is the dispenser of graces: "Let us seek for graces, and let us seek them through Mary." For the same Saint assures us that it is the will of God, that not a single grace should be dealt to us except through the hands of Mary: "God has willed us to receive nothing that has not passed through the hands of Mary." [33]

Affections and Prayers

O Jesus, My Redeemer, I trust in Thy Blood, that Thou hast forgiven me all my offences against Thee; and I fondly hope to come one day to bless Thee for it eternally in Heaven: The mercies of the Lord I will sing forever. [34] I plainly see now that I have repeatedly fallen in times past from the want of entreating Thee for holy perseverance. I earnestly beg Thee at this present moment to grant me perseverance: "Never suffer me to be separated from Thee." And I purpose to make this prayer to Thee always; but especially when I am tempted to offend Thee, I indeed make this resolution and promise; but what will it profit me thus to resolve and promise, if Thou dost not give me the grace to run and cast myself at Thy feet? By the merits, then, of Thy sacred Passion, oh, grant me this grace, in all my necessities to have recourse to Thee.

O Mary, my Queen, and my Mother, I beseech thee, by thy tender love for Jesus Christ. to procure me the grace of always fleeing for succor, as long as I live, to thy blessed Son and to thee.

II.

Desolations.

St. Francis de Sales says: "It is a mistake to estimate devotions by the consolations which we feel. True devotion in the way of God consists in having a determined will to execute all that is pleasing to God." [36]

Almighty God is wont to make use of dryness to draw closer to Him His most cherished souls. Attachment to our own inordinate inclinations is the greatest obstacle to true union with God; and when, therefore, God intends to draw a soul to His perfect love, He endeavors to detach her from all affection to created goods. Thus, His first care is to deprive her of temporal goods, of worldly pleasures, of property, honors, friends, relatives, and bodily health; by the like means of losses, troubles, neglects, bereavements, and infirmities, He extirpates by degrees all earthly attachment, in order that the affections may be set on Him alone.

With a view to produce a fondness for spiritual things, God regales the soul at first with great consolations, with aft abundance of tears and tenderness; she is thus easily weaned from the gratifications of sense, and seeks further to mortify herself with works of penance, fasts, hair cloths, and disciplines; at this stage the director must keep a check on her, and not allow her to practice mortifications -----at least not all those for which she asks permission-----because, under the spur of this sensible devotions, a soul might easily ruin her health by indiscretion. It is a subtle artifice of the devil, when he beholds a person giving himself up to God, and receiving the consolations and caresses which God generally gives to beginners, to do his utmost to plunge him into the performance of immoderate penances, so as utterly to destroy his health; so that afterwards, by reason of bodily weakness, he not only gives up the mortifications, but prayer, Communion, and all exercises of devotion, and eventually sinks back into his old way of living. On this account, the director should be very sparing in allowing mortifications to those who are only just entering upon the spiritual life, and who desire to practice bodily mortifications; let him exhort them to practice rather interior mortification, by bearing patiently with affronts and contradictions, by obedience to Superiors, by bridling the curiosity to see, to hear, and the like; and let him tell them, that when they have acquired the good habit of practicing these interior mortifications, they will then be sufficiently perfect to proceed to the external ones. For the rest, it is a serious error to say, as some say, that external mortifications are of little or no use. Without doubt, interior mortification is most requisite for perfection; but it does not follow from this that external mortifications are unnecessary. St. Vincent of Paul declared that the person who does not practice external mortifications will be neither mortified interiorly nor exteriorly. And St. John of the Cross declared that the director who despised external mortifications was unworthy of confidence, even though he should work miracles.

But to come back to our point. The soul then, in the commencement of her conversion to God, tastes the sweetness of those sensible consolations with which God seeks to allure her, and by them to wean her from earthly pleasures; she breaks off her attachment to creatures, and becomes attached to God. Still, her attachment is imperfect, because it is fostered more by that sensibility of spiritual consolations than by the real wish to do what is pleasing to God; and she deceives herself by believing that the greater the pleasure she feels in her devotions, the more she loves Almighty God. The consequence of this is, that if this food of spiritual consolations is stopped, by her being taken from her ordinary exercises of devotion, and employed in other works of obedience, charity, or duties of her state, she is disturbed, and takes it greatly to heart: and this is a universal defect in our miserable human nature, to seek our own satisfaction in all that we do. Or again, when she no longer finds this sweet relish of devotion in her exercises, she either forsakes them, or lessens them; and continuing to lessen them from day to day, she at length omits them entirely. And this misfortune befalls many souls who, when called by Almighty God to love Him, enter upon the way of perfection, and if spiritual sweetness lasts, make a certain progress; but alas! When this is no longer tasted, they leave off all, and resume their former ways. But it is of the highest importance to be fully persuaded that the love of God and perfection do not consist in feelings of tenderness and consolation, but in overcoming self-love, and in following the Divine will. St. Francis de Sales says: "God is as worthy of our love when He afflicts us as when He consoles us."

Amid these consolations, it requires no remarkable degree of virtue to forego sensual delights, and to endure affronts and contradictions. The soul in the midst of these sweetness can endure all things; but this endurance comes far more frequently from those sensible consolations than from the strength of true love of God. On this account the Lord, with a view to giving her a solid foundation in virtue, retires from her, and deprives her of that sensible devotion, that He may rid her of all attachment to self-love, which was fed by such consolations. And hence it happens, that whereas formerly she felt a joy in making acts of offering, of confidence, and of love, now that the vein of consolations is dried up, she makes these acts with coldness and painful effort; and finds a weariness in the most pious exercises, in her prayers, spiritual readings, and Communions; she even finds in them nothing but darkness and fears, and all seems lost to her. She prays and prays again, and is overwhelmed with sadness, because God seems to have abandoned her.

Let us come now to the practice of what we are to do on our part in the like circumstances. When Almighty God in His mercy deigns to console us with His loving visitations, and to let us feel the presence of His grace, it is not good to reject the Divine consolations, as some false mystics advise let us thankfully receive them; but let us beware of settling down on them and seeking delight in those feelings of spiritual tenderness. St. John of the Cross calls this a "spiritual gluttony," which is faulty and displeasing to God. Let us strive in such moments to banish from our mind the sensible enjoyment of these sweetness: and let us be especially on our guard against supposing that these favors are a token of our standing better with God than others; for such a thought of vanity would oblige God to withdraw Himself from us altogether, and to leave us in our miseries. We must certainly at such times return most fervent thanks to God, because such spiritual consolations are signal gifts of the Divine bounty to our souls, far greater than all the riches and honors of this world; but let us not seek then to regale ourselves on these sensible sweetness but let us rather humble ourselves by the remembrance of the sins of our past life. For the rest, we must consider this loving treatment as the pure result of the goodness of God; and that perhaps it is sent as the forerunner of some great tribulation soon to befall us, in order that we may be strengthened by these consolations to endure all with patience and resignation. We should therefore take the occasion of offering ourselves to suffer every pain, internal or external, that may happen to us,---every illness, every persecution, every spiritual desolation, saying: O my Lord, I am here before Thee; do with me, and with all that belongs to me, whatever Thou wilt; grant me the grace to love Thee and perfectly to accomplish Thy holy will, and I ask no more!

When a soul is morally certain of being in the grace of God, although she may be deprived of worldly pleasures, as well as of those which come from God, she nevertheless rests satisfied with her state, conscious, as she is, of loving God, and of being loved by Him. But God, Who wishes to see her purified and divested of all sensible satisfaction, in order to unite her entirely to Himself by means of pure love, what does He do? He puts her in the crucible of desolation, which is more painful to bear than the most severe trials, whether internal or external; she is left in a state of uncertainty if she be in the grace of God or not, and in the dense darkness that shrouds her, there seems no prospect of her ever more finding God. Almighty God, moreover, will sometimes permit her to be assailed by violent sensual temptations, accompanied by irregular movements of the inferior part, or perhaps by thoughts of unbelief, of despair, and even of hatred of God, when she imagines herself cast off by Him, and that He no longer hears her prayers. And as, on the one hand, the suggestions of the devil are vehement, and the motions of concupiscence are excited, and, on the other, the soul finds herself in this great darkness, she can no longer sufficiently distinguish whether she properly resists or yields to the temptations, though her will resolutely refuses all consent. Her fears of having lost God are thus very much increased; and from her fancied infidelity in struggling against the temptations, she thinks herself deservedly abandoned by God. The saddest of all calamities seems to have befallen her,---to be able no longer to love God, and to be hated by Him. St. Teresa passed through all these trials and declares that during them solitude had no charms for her, but, on the contrary, filled her with horror, while prayer was changed for her into a perfect hell.

When a soul that loves God finds herself in this state, she must not lose courage; and neither must he who directs her become alarmed. Those sensual movements, those temptations against faith, those feelings of distrust, and those attacks which urge her to hate Almighty God, are fears, are tortures of the soul, are efforts of the enemy; but they are not voluntary, and therefore they are not sins. The sincere lover of Jesus Christ resists valiantly on such occasions and withholds all consent to such suggestions; but because of the darkness which envelops her, she knows not how to distinguish, her soul is thrown into confusion, and the privation of the presence of Divine grace makes her fearful and sad. But it can be soon discovered that in these souls, thus tried by God, all is dread and apprehension, but not truth: only ask them, even in their state of desolation, whether they would willingly commit one single deliberate venial sin; they will answer, that they are ready to suffer not one, but a thousand deaths, rather than be guilty of such displeasure to Almighty God. It is necessary, therefore, to make this distinction, that it is one thing to perform an act of virtue, such as to repel a temptation, to trust in God, to love God, and to will what He wills; and it is another thing to have the consciousness of really making these good acts. This consciousness of doing good contributes to our pleasure; but profit consists in the first point, that is, in doing good. With the first God is satisfied and deprives the soul of the latter---that is, of the consciousness of doing good, in order thus to remove from her all self-satisfaction, which adds nothing to the merit of the action; for our Lord seeks more our real advantage than our own satisfaction. St. John of the Cross wrote the following words of comfort to a desolate soul: "You were never in a better state than at present; for you were never so deeply humbled, and so cut off from all attachment to this world, and at the same time you were never so thoroughly impressed with the conviction of your own wickedness. Neither were you ever so divested and purified of all self-seeking as now." [36] Let us, then, not believe that when we feel a greater tenderness of devotion, we are more beloved by God; for perfection does not consist in that, but in the mortification of our own will, and in its union with the will of God.

Wherefore, in this state of desolation the soul must not heed the devil, when he suggests that God has abandoned her; nor must she leave off prayer. This is the object at which the devil is aiming, in order afterwards to drag her down some precipice. St. Teresa writes: "The Lord proves His true lovers by dryness and temptations. What though the dryness should be of lifelong duration, let the soul never relax in prayer; the time will arrive when all will be abundantly repaid." [37] In such a state of suffering, a person should humble himself by the reflection that his offences against God are undeserving of any milder treatment: he should humble himself, and be fully resigned to the Divine will, saying: O my Lord, behold me at Thy feet; if it be Thy will that I should remain thus desolate and afflicted for my whole life, and even for all eternity, only grant me Thy grace and the gift of Thy love, and do with me whatever Thou wilt. It will be useless then, and perhaps a source of greater disquiet, to wish to assure yourself that you are in the grace of God, and that what you experience is only a trial, and not abandonment on the part of God. At such times it is not the will of God that you should have this assurance; and He so wills it for your greater advantage, in order that you may humble yourself the more, and increase your prayers and acts of confidence in His mercy. You desire to see, and God wills that you should not see. For the rest, St. Francis de Sales says: "The resolution not to consent to any sin, however small, is a sure sign that we are in God's grace." [38] But a soul in profound desolation cannot even clearly discern this resolution; nevertheless, in such a state she must not aim at feeling what she wills; it is enough to will with the point of the will. In this manner she should entirely abandon herself into the arms of the Divine goodness. Oh, how do such acts of confidence and resignation ravish the heart of God, when made in the midst of the darkness of desolation! Ah, let us simply trust in a God, Who (as St. Teresa says) loves us far better than we love ourselves.

Let these souls, then, so dear to God, and who are resolutely determined to belong entirely to Him, take comfort, although at the same time they see themselves deprived of every consolation. Their desolation is a sign of their being very acceptable to God, and that He has for them a place prepared in His heavenly kingdom, which overflows with consolations as full as they are lasting, And let them hold for certain, that the more they are afflicted in the present life, so much the more they shall be consoled in eternity: According to the multitude of my sorrows in my heart, Thy comforts have given joy to my soul. [39]

Example.

For the encouragement of souls in desolation, I will here mention what is related in the life of St. Jane Frances de Chantal.

For the space of forty years, she was tormented by the most fearful interior trials, by temptations, by fears of being in enmity with God, and of being even quite forsaken by Him. Her afflictions were so excruciating and unremitting, that she declared her sole ray of comfort came from the thought of death. Moreover, she said: "I am so furiously assaulted that I know not where to hide my poor soul. I seem at times on the point of losing all patience, and of giving up all as utterly lost." "The tyrant of temptation is so relentless," she says, "that any hour of the day I would gladly barter it with the loss of my life; and sometimes it happens that I can neither eat nor sleep." [40] During the last eight or nine years of her life, her temptations became still more violent. Mother de Chatel said that her saintly Mother de Chantal suffered a continual interior martyrdom night and day, at prayer, at work, and even during sleep; so that she felt the deepest compassion for her. The Saint endured assaults against every virtue (except chastity), and had likewise to contend with doubts, darkness, and disgust. Sometimes God would withdraw all lights from her, and seem indignant with her, and just on the point of expelling her from Him; so that terror drove her to look in some other direction for relief: but failing to find any, she was obliged to return to look on God, and to abandon herself to His mercy. She seemed at each moment ready to yield to the violence of her temptations. The Divine assistance did not indeed forsake her; but it seemed to her to have done so, since, instead of finding satisfaction in anything, she found only weariness and anguish in prayer, in reading spiritual books, in Communion, and in all other exercises of piety. Her sole resource in this state of dereliction was to look upon God, and to let Him do His will. The Saint said: "In all my abandonments my mere life is a new cross to me, and my incapability of action adds considerably to its heaviness." And it was therefore that she compared herself to a sick person overwhelmed with sufferings, unable to turn from one side to the other, speechless, so as not to be able to express his ills, and blind, so as not to discern whether the attendants are administering to him medicine or poison. And then, weeping bitterly, she added, "I seem to be without faith, without hope, and without love for my God." Nevertheless, the Saint maintained throughout her serenity of countenance and affability in conversation, and kept her looks fixedly bent towards God, in the bosom of Whose blessed will she constantly reposed. Wherefore St. Francis de Sales, who was her director, and knew well what an object of predilection her beautiful soul was to Almighty God, wrote thus of her: "Her heart resembled a deaf musician, who, though he may sing most exquisitely, can derive no pleasure from it himself." And to herself he wrote as follows: "You must endeavor to serve your Savior solely through love of His blessed will, utterly deprived of consolations, and overwhelmed by a deluge of fears and sadness." [41] It is thus that the Saints are formed:

> "Long did the chisels ring around,
> Long did the mallet's blows rebound,
> Long work'd the head and toil'd the hand,
> Ere stood thy stones as now they stand."-----Offic. Dedic. eccl.

The Saints of whom the Church sings are precisely these choice stones, which are reduced to shapeliness and beauty by the strokes of the chisel,-----that is, by temptations, by fears, by darkness, and other torments, internal and external,-----till at length they are made worthy to be enthroned in the blessed kingdom of Paradise.

Affections and Prayers

O Jesus, my hope, my love and only love of my soul, I deserve not Thy consolations and sweet visitations; keep them for those innocent souls that have always loved Thee; sinner that I am, I do not deserve them, nor do I ask for them: this only do I ask, give me grace to love Thee, to accomplish Thy adorable will during my whole life; and then dispose of me as Thou please! Unhappy me! far other darkness, other terrors, other abandonments would be due to the outrages which I have done Thee: Hell were my just award, where, separated from Thee forever, and totally abandoned by Thee, I should shed tears eternally, without ever being able to love Thee more. But no, my Jesus, I accept of every punishment; only spare me this. Thou art deserving of an infinite love; Thou hast placed me under an excessive obligation of loving Thee; oh, no, I cannot trust myself to live and not love Thee! I do love Thee, my sovereign good; I love Thee with my whole heart; I love Thee more than myself; I love Thee and have no other desire than to love Thee. I own that this my good-will is the pure effect of Thy grace; but do Thou, O my Lord, perfect Thy Own work; withdraw not Thy helping hand till death! Oh, never for a moment leave me in my own hands; give me strength to vanquish temptations and to overcome myself; and for this end give me grace always to have, recourse to Thee! I wish to belong wholly to Thee! I give Thee my body, my soul, my will, and my liberty; I will no longer live for myself, but for Thee alone, my Creator, my Redeemer, my love, and my all: my God and my all. I desire to become a Saint, and I hope this of Thee. Afflict me as Thou wilt, deprive me of all: only deprive me not of Thy grace and of Thy love.

O Mary, the hope of sinners, great is thy power with God; I confide fully in thy intercession: I entreat thee by thy love of Jesus Christ, help me, and make me a Saint!

14

— ✦ —

ABSTRACT OF VIRTUES TREATED IN THIS WORK, TO BE PRACTICED BY HIM WHO LOVES JESUS CHRIST

I. We must patiently endure the tribulations of this life-----ill-health, sorrows, poverty, losses, bereavement of kindred, affronts, persecutions, and all that is disagreeable. Let us invariably look on the trials of this world as signs of God's love towards us, and of His desire to save us in the world to come. And let us, moreover, be fully persuaded that the involuntary mortifications which God Himself sends us are far more pleasing to Him than those which are the fruit of our own choice.

In sickness let us endeavor to resign ourselves entirely to the will of God; no devout exercise is more acceptable to Him than this. If at such times we are unable to meditate, let us fix our eyes on our crucified Lord, and offer Him our sufferings in union with all that He endured for us upon the Cross. And when we are told that we are about to die, let us accept the tidings with tranquility and in the spirit of sacrifice; that is, with the desire to die, to give pleasure to Jesus Christ: it was the like desire that gave all the merit to the death of the Martyrs. We should then say: O Lord, behold me here with no other will but Thine Own blessed will; I am willing to suffer as much as Thou pleases; I wish to die whenever Thou wilt. Nor should we then wish to have our life prolonged, to do penance for our sins: to accept death with perfect resignation outweighs all other penance.

We must likewise practice conformity to the will of God in bearing poverty and the various inconveniences which accompany it: cold, hunger, fatigue, contempt, and scorn.

Nor should we be less resigned to losses, whether of property or of relatives and friends, on whom our ease and happiness depended. Let us acquire the good habit of saying in every adversity: God hath so willed it, and so I will it likewise. And at the death of our relatives, instead of wasting time in fruitless tears, let us employ it in praying for their souls; and offer to Jesus Christ, in their behalf, the pain of our bereavement.

Let us, moreover, force ourselves to endure scorn and insult with patience and tranquility. Let us answer in terms of outrage and injury with words of gentleness; but if we feel ourselves disturbed, the best plan is to keep silent, till the mind grows tranquil. Meanwhile let us not be fretfully speaking to others of the affront we have received, but in silence offer it to Jesus Christ, Who endured so much for us.

II. Behave kindly to all, to Superiors and inferiors, to the high-born and peasant, to relatives and strangers; but more especially to the poor and infirm, and, above all, to those who regard us with an evil eye.

Gentleness in the correction of faults is more efficacious than any other means or reasons that may be employed. Be therefore on your guard against correcting in a fit of passion; for then harshness is sure to be mingled with it, either in word or action. Beware likewise of correcting the person in fault while he is excited; for in like cases the result is exasperation instead of improvement.

III. Envy not the great ones of this world their riches, honors, dignities, or applause, given them by men; but envy rather those who most love Jesus Christ, who undoubtedly enjoy greater happiness than the first monarchs of the earth. Return thanks to the Lord for enlightening you to discover the vanity of all worldly things, for the sake of which so many unhappily perish.

IV. In all our actions and thoughts let us seek only the pleasure of Almighty God, and not our private satisfaction; and let us therefore lay aside all disquietude when our efforts are attended with failure. And when we succeed, let us be no less cautious against seeking the thanks and approbation of men; should they murmur against us, let us pay no attention to this; our consolation will be to have striven to please God, and not men.

V. The chief means of perfection are:

1. To avoid all deliberate sin, however small. Should we, however, happen unfortunately to commit a fault, let us refrain from becoming angry and impatient with ourselves: we must, on such occasions, quietly repent of it; and while we make an act of love to Jesus Christ, and beg His help, we must promise Him not to repeat the fault.

2. To have an earnest desire to acquire the perfection of the Saints, and to suffer all things to please Jesus Christ; and if we have not this desire, to beseech Jesus Christ, through His bounty, to grant it us; since, as long as we do not feel a sincere desire of becoming Saints, we shall never make one step forward in the way of perfection.

3. To have a firm resolution of arriving at perfection: whoever is wanting in this resolution, works but languidly, and in the occasion does not overcome his repugnance; whereas a resolute soul, by the Divine aid, which never fails her, surmounts every obstacle.

4. To make daily two hours' or at least one hour's mental prayer; and, except in case of urgent necessity, never to relinquish it for the sake of any weariness, dryness, or trouble that we may experience.

5. To frequent Holy Communion several times a week, it is well to seek the counsel of our director, "in order that the practice may be carried out with greater prudence and more abundant merit." The same rule holds good regarding external mortifications, such as fasting, wearing the cilice, taking the discipline, and the rest; mortifications of this kind, when practiced without obedience to our spiritual director, will either destroy health or produce vainglory. Hence it is necessary for each one to have his own director, so that all may be regulated in obedience to him.

6. To pray continually, by having recourse to Jesus Christ in all our necessities, by invoking likewise the intercession of our Angel Guardian, of our Holy Patrons, and most particularly of the Mother of God through whose hands Almighty God bestows all graces upon us. It has already been shown, at the end of Chapter IV, that our welfare entirely depends on prayer. We must especially not pass a day without begging God to grant us the gift of perseverance in His grace; whosoever asks for this perseverance obtains it, but he that does not ask for it obtains it not, and is damned: we must pray, too, that Jesus Christ may grant us His holy love and perfect conformity with His Divine will. Neither should we forget to pray for every grace through the merits of Jesus Christ. We must first make

these prayers when We rise in the morning, and afterwards repeat them in our meditation, at Holy Communion, at the visit to the Blessed Sacrament, and again in the evening at the examination of conscience. We must particularly cry to God for help in the time of temptation, and more especially in temptations against purity, when we should not cease to call for succor on the holy names of Jesus and Mary. He that prays, conquers; he that prays not, is conquered.

VI. With respect to humility, not to pride ourselves on riches, honors, high birth, talents, or any other natural advantage, and still less on any spiritual gift, reflecting that all are the gifts of God. To consider ourselves the worst of all, and consequently to delight in being despised by others; and not to act as some do, who declare themselves the worst of men, and at the same time wish to be treated as the best. Moreover, to receive corrections humbly, and without attempts to excuse ourselves, and this even though blamed wrongfully; except when to defend ourselves would be necessary in order to prevent others being scandalized.

Much more ought we to banish all desire of appearing in public, and of being honored by the world. The maxim of St. Francis should never be out of our sight: "We are just what we are before God." It would be still worse for a religious to covet posts of honor and superiority in his community. The true honor of a religious is to be the humblest of all; and he is the humblest of all who most joyfully embraces humiliations.

VII. Detach your heart from all creatures. Whoever continues bound by the slightest fondness to things of earth can never rise to a perfect union with God.

To detach ourselves especially from an undue affection for our relatives. It was said by St. Philip Neri, that "whatever affection we bestow on creatures is so much taken from God." [1] In deciding on a state of life we must be quite unbiased by the advice of parents, who generally keep their own interests in view, rather than our real welfare.

Cast away all considerations of human respect, and of the vain esteem of men; and, above all, be detached from self-will. We must leave all, to gain all. "All for all," writes Thomas à Kempis. [2]

VIII. Not to give way to anger, whatever happens; but if perchance the sparks of passion are suddenly lighted in our breasts, let us call on God, and refrain from acting or speaking till we are sure that our anger is appeased. We shall find it of great service to arm ourselves in prayer against every chance of irritation that may befall us, in order not then to give way to culpable resentment; we should always remember that saying of St. Francis de Sales: "I never remember to have been angry with. out afterwards regretting it."

IX. All sanctity consists in loving God, and all love of God consists in doing His blessed will. We must, therefore, bow with resignation to all the dispositions of Divine Providence without reserve; and so cheerfully submit to the adversity as well as prosperity which God sends, to the state of life in which God places us, to the sort of health which God bestows on us: and this should be the grand aim of all our prayers, namely, that God would enable us to fulfill His holy will in all things. And to be certain of the Divine will, the religious must depend on obedience to his Superior, and those who are in the world to their confessor; for nothing is more certain than that saying of St. Philip Neri: "We shall have no account to render to God of what is done through obedience." Which is to be understood, of course, as long as there is no evident sin in the command.

X. There are two remedies against temptations: resignation and prayer. Resignation, for though temptations do not come from God, yet He permits them for our good.

Wherefore beware of yielding to vexation, however annoying the temptations may be; be resigned to the will of God, Who allows them; and take up the arms of prayer, which are the most powerful and the most certain to overcome our enemies. Bad thoughts, however filthy and abominable, are not sins; it is only consenting to them which makes the sin. We shall never be overcome if we call on the holy names of Jesus and Mary. During the assaults of temptation, it is of service to renew our resolution to suffer death rather than to offend God; it is also a good practice repeatedly to sign ourselves with the Sign of the Cross, and with holy water; it is of great help, too, to discover the temptation to the confessor. But prayer is the most necessary remedy, and continual cries for help to Jesus and Mary.

XI. Then as to spiritual desolations, there are two acts in which we ought principally to exercise ourselves: 1st, to humble ourselves, with the sincere avowal that we deserve no better treatment; 2nd, to resign ourselves to the will of God, and to abandon ourselves into the arms of His Divine goodness. When God favors us with consolations, let us prepare ourselves for coming trials, which generally follow consolations. If it please God to leave us in desolation, let us be humble and fully resigned to His Divine will, and we shall thus reap far greater advantage from desolations than from consolations.

XII. To live always well, we must store up deeply in our mind's certain general maxims of eternal life, such as the following:

All passes away in this life, whether it be joy or sorrow; but in eternity nothing passes away.

What good is all the greatness of this world at the hour of death?

All that comes from God, whether it be adverse or prosperous, all is good, and is for our welfare.

We must leave all, to gain all.

There is no peace to be found without God.

To love God and save one's soul is the one thing needful.

We need only be afraid of sin.

If God be lost, all is lost.

He that desires nothing in this world is master of the whole world.

He that prays is saved, and he that prays not is damned.

Let me die and give God pleasure.

God is cheap at any cost.

Every pain is slight to him who has deserved Hell.

He bears all who looks on Jesus crucified.

Everything becomes a pain that is not done for God.

Whoever wishes for God alone is rich in every good.

Happy the man who can say: "My Jesus, I desire Thee alone, and nothing more!"

He that loves God, finds pleasure in everything; he that loves not God, finds no true pleasure in anything.

15

— • —

FOOTNOTES

Introduction:

1. "Ipse enim Pater amat vos, quia vos me amastis."—John, xvi. 27.

2. Spirit, p. 1, ch. 25.

3. "Super omnia, ... charitatem habete, quod est vinculum perfectionis."—Col. iii. 14.

4. "Ama, et fac quod vis."

5. "In charitate perpetua dilexi te."—Jer. xxxi. 3.

6. "Ab alio amatore præventa sum."

7. "In funiculis Adam traham eos, in vinculis charitatis."—Osee, xi. 4

8. "Cœlum et terra et omnia mihi dicunt, ut te amem."—Conf. B. 10, c. 6.

9. "Sic enim Deus dilexit mundum, ut Filium unigenitum daret." John, iii. 16.

10. "Propter nimiam charitatem suam qua dilexit nos, et cum essemus mortui peccatis, convivificavit nos in Christo."—Eph. ii. 4.

11. "Qui etiam proprio Filio suo non pepercit, sed pro nobis omni bus tradidit illum: quomodo non etiam cum illo omnia nobis donavit?"—Rom. viii. 32.

12. "Dilexit me, et tradidit semetipsum pro me."—Gal. ii. 20.

13. "Et Verbum caro factum est."—John, i. 14.

14. "Exinanivit semetipsum formam servi accipiens, ... et habitu inventus ut hom o."—Phil. ii. 7.

15. "Humiliavit semetipsum, factus obediens usque ad mortem, mortem autem crucis."—Phil. ii. 8.

16. "Dilexit nos, et tradidit semetipsum pro nobis."—Eph. v. 2.

17. "Charitas Christi urget nos."—2 Cor. v. 14.

18. Love of God, B. 7, c. 8.

19. Love of God, B. 12, c. 13.

20. "Baptismo habeo baptizari; et quomodo coarctor usquedum perficiatur!"—Luke, xii. 50.

21. "Sciens Jesus quia venit hora ejus, ut transeat ex hoc mundo ad Patrem, cum dilexisset suos, ... in finem dilexit eos."—John, xiii. 1.

22. "Quis hoc fecit?—Fecit amor, dignitatis nescius."—In Cant. s. 61.

23. "Vidimus Sapientiam amoris nimietate infatuatam."—Serm. de Nat. D.

24. "Extasim facit divinus amor."—De Div. Nom. c. 4.

25. "Vulnera, corda saxea vulnerantia, et mentes congelatas inflammantia."—Stim. div. am. p. 1, c. 1.

26. "Charitas Christi urget nos."—2 Cor. v. 14.

27. "Ut cognoscat mundus quia diligo Patrem, ... surgite, eamus."—John, xiv. 31.

28. "In hoc enim Christus mortuus est et resurrexit, ut et mortuorum et vivorum dominetur."—Rom. xiv. 9.

29. Disc. on the Love of God.

30. De Duob. Præc. c. 4.

31. Epist. 20.

32. "Si quis non amat Dominum nostrum Jesum Christum, sit anathema."—1 Cor.
xvi. 22.

33. "Si vis proficere, quotidie mediteris Domini passionem; nihil enim in anima ita
operatur universalem sanctimoniam, sicut meditatio passionis Christi."

34. "Magis meretur vel unam lacrymam emittens ob memoriam passionis Christi,
quam si qualibet anni hebdomada in pane et aqua jejunaret."—Rosar. p. 2, s.
15.

35. "Sciens Jesus quia venit hora ejus, ut transeat ex hoc mundo ad Patrem, cum
dilexisset suos qui erant in mundo, in finem dilexit eos."—John, xiii. I.

36. "Quæ in fine in signum amicitiæ celebrantur, firmius memoriæ imprimuntur, et
cariora tenentur."—T. ii, s. 54, a. i, c. 1.

37. "Totum tibi dedit, nihil sibi reliquit."

38. "Divitias divini sui erga homines amoris velut effudit."—Sess. xiii. c. 2.

39. "In qua nocte tradebatur, accepit panem, et gratias agens fregit, et dixit: Accipite
et manducate; hoc est corpus meum."—1 Cor. xi. 23.

40. "In illo fervoris excessu, quando paratus erat pro nobis mori, ab excessu amoris
majus opus agere coactus est, quam umquam operatus fuit, dare nobis corpus
in cibum."—Loco cit.

41. "Sacramentum charitatis, Pignus charitatis."

42. "Amor amorum."

43. "In quo ... futuræ gloriæ nobis pignus datur."

44. Isa. xii. 4.

45. "Nonne videtur insania: Manducate meam carnem, bibite meum san-
guinem?"—In Ps. xxxiii. en. 1.

46. "Quomodo potest hic nobis carnem suam dare ad manducandum?—Durus est hic sermo; et quis potest eum audire?"—John, vi. 53, 61.

47. "Accipite et manducate; hoc est corpus meum."

48. "Desiderio desideravi hoc pascha manducare vobiscum."—Luke, xxii. 15.

49. "Flagrantissimæ charitatis est vox hæc."—De Tr. Chr. Ag. c. 2.

50. "Venite, comedite panem meum, et bibite vinum quod miscui vobis."—Prov. ix. 5.

51. "Comedite, amici, et bibite."—Cant. v. i.

52. "Qui manducat meam carnem, ... habet vitam æternam. Qui manducat hunc panem, vivet in æternum."—John, vi. 55, 59.

53. "Nisi manducaveritis carnem Filii hominis, ... non habebitis vitam in vobis." —John, vi. 54.

54. "Amantes desiderant ex ambobus fieri unum."—1. 2, q. 28, a. 1.

55. "En ipse stat post parietem nostrum respiciens per fenestras, prospiciens per cancellos."—Cant. ii. 9.

56. "Qui manducat meam carnem, ... in me manet, et ego in illo."—John, vi. 57.

57. Introd. p. 2, ch. 21.

58. "Semetipsum nobis immiscuit, ut unum quid simus; ardenter enim amantium hoc est."—Ad pop. Ant. hom. 61.

59. "O quam mirabilis est dilectio tua, Domine Jesu, qui tuo corpori taliter nos incorporari voluisti, ut tecum unum cor et unam animam haberemus insepa-rabiliter colligatam!"—De Inc. div. am. c. 5.

60. "Ultimus gradus amoris est, cum se dedit nobis in cibum; quia dedit se nobis ad omnimodam unionem, sicut cibus et cibans invicem uniuntur."—T. ii. s. 54, a. 4, c. i.

61. Introd. p. 2, ch. 21.

62. "Frequens accessus (ad Eucharistiam) confessariorum judicio est relinquendus, qui, ... laicis negotiatoribus et conjugatis, quod prospicient eorum saluti profuturum, id illis præscribere debebunt."

63. "Omnia dedit ei Pater in manus."—John, xiii. 3.

64. "Venerunt mihi omnia bona pariter cum illa."—Wisd. vii. 11.

65. Eucharistia maximam vim habet perficiendæ sanctitatis."

66. "Antidotum quo liberemur a culpis quotidianis, et a peccatis mortalibus præs ervemur."—Sess. xiii. c. 2.

67. P. 3, q. 79, a. 4.

68. "Per crucis mysterium, eripuit nos a potestate peccati; per Eucharistiæ sacramentum, liberat nos a voluntate peccandi."—De Alt. Myst. l. 4, c. 44.

69. "Deus charitas est."—1 John, iv. 8.

70. "Ignis consumens est."—Deut. iv. 24.

71. "Ignem veni mittere in terram; et quid volo, nisi ut accendatur?"—Luke, xii. 49.

72. "Carbo est Eucharistia, quæ nos inflammat, ut tamquam leones ignem spirantes ab illa mensa recedamus, facti diabolo terribiles."—Ad pop. Ant. hom. 61.

73. "Introduxit me in cellam vinariam, ordinavit in me charitatem."—Cant. ii. 4.

74. "Fulcite me floribus, stipate me malis, quia amore langueo."—Cant. ii. 5.

75. "Licet tepide, tamen confidens de misericordia Dei accedat; tanto magis æger necesse habet requirere medicum, quanto magis senserit se ægrotum."—De Prof. rel. l. 2, c. 77.

76. Introd. p. 2. ch. 21.

77. Spir. Grat. l. 3, c. 22.

78. "In manus tuas commendo spiritum meum; redemisti me, Domine Deus veritatis."—Ps. xxx. 6.

79. "Vere languores nostros ipse tulit, et dolores nostros ipse portavit."—Isa. liii. 4.

80. "Delens quod adversus nos erat chirographum decreti, quod erat contrarium nobis, et ipsum tulit de medio, affigens illud cruci."—Col. ii. 14.

81. "Accessistis ad ... Mediatorem Jesum, et sanguinis aspersionem melius loquentem quam Abel."—Heb. xii. 22, 24.

82. "Pater ... omne judicium dedit Filio."—John, v. 22.

83. "Quis est qui condemnet? Christus Jesus, qui mortuus est, ... qui etiam interpellat pro nobis."—Rom. viii. 34.

84. "Quid times, peccator? Quomodo te damnabit pœnitentem, qui moritur ne damneris? Quomodo te abjiciet redeuntem, qui de cœlo venit quærere te?"—Tr. de Adv. D.

85. "Curramus ad propositum nobis certamen, aspicientes in Auctorem fidei et consummatorem Jesum, qui, proposito sibi gaudio, sustinuit crucem, confusione contempta."—Heb. xii. 1, 2.

86. Life, ch. 25.

87. Life, ch. 8.

88. "Fiducialiter agam, immobiliter sperans nihil ad salutem necessarium ab eo negandum, qui tanta pro mea salute fecit et pertulit."

89. "Adeamus ergo cum fiducia ad thronum gratiæ, ut misericordiam consequamur, et gratiam inveniamus in auxilio opportune."—Heb. iv. 16.

90. "In omnibus divites facti estis in illo, ... ita ut nihil vobis desit in ulla gratia."—1 Cor. i. 5, 7.

91. "Ampliora adepti sumus per Christi gratiam, quam per diaboli amiseramus invidiam."—De Asc. s. 1.

92. "Non sicut delictum, ita et donum: ... ubi abundavit delictum, superabundavit gratia."—Rom. v. 15.

93. "Amen, amen, dico vobis: si quid petieritis Patrem in nomine meo, dabit vobis."—John, xvi. 23.

94. "Pro nobis omnibus tradidit illum: quomodo non etiam cum illo omnia nobis donavit?"—Rom. viii. 32.

95. "Dives in omnes qui invocant illum."—Ibid. x. 12.

96. "O mors! ero mors tua."—Osee, xiii. 14.

97. "Pater! quos dedisti mihi, volo ut, ubi sum ego, et illi sint mecum."—John, xvii. 24.

98. "Numquid oblivisci potest mulier infantem suum, ut non misereatur filio uteri sui? et si illa oblita fuerit, ego tamen non obliviscar tui."—Isa. xlix. 15.

99. Part 2, Ep. 48.

100. "Non ad aliud amat, nisi ut ametur."—In Cant. s. 83.

101. "Et nunc, Israel, quid Dominus Deus tuus petit a te, nisi ut timeas Dominum Deum tuum, ... et diligas eum?"—Deut. x. 12.

102. "Diliges Dominum Deum tuum ex toto corde tuo."—Deut. vi. 5.

103. "Plenitude legis est dilectio."—Rom. xiii. 10.

104. "Completio legis."

105. Love of God, B. 7, ch. 8.

106. "Pro omnibus mortuus est Christus, ut et qui vivunt, jam non sibi vivant, sed ei qui pro ipsis mortuus est."—2 Cor. v. 15.

107. "Gratiam fidejussoris ne obliviscaris; dedit enim pro te animam suam."—Ecclus. xxix, 20.

108. "Accipite et manducate; hoc est corpus meum: ... hoc facite in meam commemorationem. ... Quotiescumque enim manducabitis panem hunc, ... mortem Domini annuntiabitis."—1 Cor. xi. 24.

109. "Deus qui nobis sub Sacramento mirabili passionis ture memoriam reliquisti. ..."

110. "O sacrum convivium, in quo Christus sumilur, recolitur memoria passionis ejus! ..."

111. "Testis crux, testes dolores, testis amara mors quam pro te sustinuit."—Dom. 17 p. Pent. conc. 3.

112. "Magna res amor."—In Cant. s. 83.

113. "Infinitus enim thesaurus est hominibus, quo qui usi sunt, participes facti sunt amicitiæ Dei."—Wisd. vii. 14.

114. "Charitas est virtus conjungens nos Deo."

115. "Ego diligentes me diligo."—Prov. viii. 17.

116. "Si quis diligit me, ... Pater meus diliget eum, et ad eum veniemus, et mansionem apud eum faciemus."—John, xiv. 23.

117. "Qui manet in charitate, in Deo manet, et Deus in eo."—1 John, iv. 16.

118. Fortis est ut mors dilectio."—Cant. viii. 6.

119. "Nihil tam durum, quod amoris igne non vincatur."—De Mor. Eccl. cat. c. 22.

120. "In eo quod amatur, aut non laboratur, aut et labor amatur."—De Bono vid. c. 21.

121. Spirit, p. 1, ch. 25.

122. "Porro unum est necessarium."—Luke, x. 42.

123. "Pone me ut signaculum super cor tuum, ut signaculum super brachium tuum."—Cant. viii. 6.

124. "Et si habuero omnem fidem, ita ut montes transferam, charitatem autem non habuero, nihil sum. Et si distribuero in cibos pauperum omnes facilitates meas; et si tradidero corpus meum, ita ut ardeam, charitatem autem non habuero, nihil mihi prodest."—1 Cor. xiii. 2, 3.

125. "Charitas patiens est, benigna est; charitas non æmulatur, non agit perperam, non inflatur, non est ambitiosa, non quærit quæ sua sunt, non irritatur; non cogitat malum, non gaudet super iniquitate, congaudet autem veritati; omnia suffert, omnia credit, omnia sperat, omnia sustinet."—1 Cor. xiii. 4–7.

Chapter 1:

1. "Homo natus de muliere, brevi vivens tempore, repletur multis miseriis."—Job, xiv. i.

2. "Una eademque tunsio bonos producit ad gloriam, malos redigit in favillam." —Serm. 52, E. B. app.

3. "Nam quos præscivit, et prædestinavit conformes fieri imaginis Filii sui."—Rom. viii. 29.

4. "Christus passus est pro nobis, vobis relinquens exemplum, ut sequamini vestigia ejus."—1 Pet. ii. 21.

5. "Despectum et novissimum virorum."—Isa. liii. 3.

6. "Quem enim diligit Dominus, castigat; flagellat autem omnem filium quem recipit."—Heb. xii. 6.

7. Life, addit.

8. Abelly, l. 3, c. 43.

9. In Phil. hom. 4.

10. In Eph. hom. 8.

11. "Patientia autem opus perfectum habet."—James, i. 4.

12. "Amicti stolis albis, et palmae in manibus eorum."—Apoc. vii. 9.

13. "Nos sine ferro esse possumus martyres, si patientiam veraciter in animo custodimus."—In Evang. hom. 35.

14. Life, addit.

15. Life, ch. 30.

16. Boll. 31 Maii. Vit. c. 7.

17. Found. ch. 31.

18. "Non sunt condignæ passiones hujus temporis ad futuram gloriam quæ revelabitur in nobis."—Rom. viii. 18.

19. "Momentaneum et leve tribulationis nostræ supra modum in sublimitate æternum gloriæ pondus operatur in nobis."—2 Cor. iv. 17.

20. "Si sustinebimus, et conregnabimus."—2 Tim. ii. 12.

21. "Qui certat in agone, non coronatur, nisi legitime certaverit."—2 Tim. ii. 5.

22. Bacci, l. 2, ch. 20.

23. Spirit, ch. 19.

24. Life, ch. 10.

25. "Tollat crucem suam quotidie, et sequatur me."—Luke, ix. 23.

26. Mont. du C. l. 2, ch. 7.

27. "Melior est patiens viro forti."–Prov. xvi. 32.

28. Spirit, ch. 4.

29. Way of Perf. ch. 37.

Chapter 2:

1. "Spiritus enim meus super mel dulcis."—Ecclus. xxiv. 27.

2. Lettre 853.

3. Lettre 786.

4. "Vince in bono malum."—Rom. xii. 21.

5. Lettre 605.

6. Abelly, l. 3, ch. 27.

7. Introd. ch. 8.

8. Mém. de la M. de Chaugy, p. 3, ch. 19.

9. "Quod si zelum amarum habetis, ... nolite gloriari."—James, iii. 14.

10. "Nescitis cujus spiritus estis."—Luke, ix. 55.

11. "Filius hominis non venit animas perdere, sed salvare."—Luke, x. 56.

12. "Mulier, ... nemo te condemnavit? ... Nec ego te condemnabo. Vade, et jam amplius noli peccare."—John, viii. 10, 11.

13. "Juda! osculo Filium hominis tradis?"—Luke, xxii. 48.

14. "Conversus Dominus respexit Petrum."—Luke, xxii. 61.

15. Abelly, 1. 3, ch. 27.

16. In Adv. D. s. 4.

17. Spirit, ch. 10.

18. "Responsio mollis frangit iram."—Prov. xv. 1.

19. Life, ch. 30.

Chapter 3:

1. "'Non æmulatur;' quia, per hoc quod in præsenti mundo nihil appetit, invidere terrenis successibus nescit."—Mor. l. 10, c. 8.

2. "Vulnerasti cor meum, soror mea Sponsa, vulnerasti cor meum in uno oculorum tuorum."—Cant. iv. 9.

3. "Quid enim mihi est in cœlo? et a te quid volui super terram? ... Deus cordis mei, et pars mea, Deus, in æternum."—Ps. lxxii. 25, 26.

4. "Sibi habeant divitias suas divites, sibi regna sua reges; nobis gloria, et possessio, et regnum, Christus est."—Ep. ad Aprum.

5. "Bene omnia fecit."—Mark, vii. 37.

6. Pucc. p. 1, ch. 58.

7. "Attendite ne justitiam vestram faciatis coram hominibus, ut videamini ab eis; alioquin mercedem non habebitis apud Patrem vestrum qui in cœlis est."—Matt. vi. i.

8. "Amen, dico vobis, receperunt mercedem suam."—Matt. vi. 5.

9. "Et qui mercedes congregavit, misit eas in sacculum pertusum."—Agg. i. 6.

10. "Euge, serve bone et fidelis: quia super pauca fuisti fidelis, super multa te constituam; intra in gaudium Domini tui."—Matt. xxv. 21.

11. "Si dignus fueris agere aliquid quod Deo placet, aliam, præter id, mercedem requiris?"—De Compunct. l. 2.

12. "Pone me ut signaculum super cor tuum, ut signaculum super brachium tuum."—Cant. viii. 6.

13. Found, ch. 12.

14. Life, ch. 2.

Chapter 4:

1. "Non agit perperam. Quia (charitas), quæ se in solum Dei amorem dilatat, quidquid a rectitudine discrepat, ignorat."—Mor. l. 10, c. 3.

2. "Charitatem habete, quod est vinculum perfectionis."—Col. iii. 14.

3. Lettre 51.

4. "Antidotum, quo liberemur a culpis quotidianis"

5. Way of Perf. ch. 42.

6. Inter. Castle, ch. 3.

7. Found, ch. 29.

8. Neque frigidus es, neque calidus; utinam frigidus esses, aut calidus! sed, quia tepidus es, ... incipiam te evomere."—Apoc. iii. 15, 16.

9. "Tepor (quia fervore defecit) in desperatione est."—Past. p. 3, adm. 35

10. "Quæ impossibilia sunt apud homines, possibilia sunt apud Deum."—Luke, xviii. 27.

11. "Vires subministrat, poenam exhibet leviorem."—De Disc. mon. c. 6.

12. "Non progredi, jam reverti est."—Ep. 17, E. B. app.

13. "Hæc est voluntas Dei, sanctificatio vestra."—1 Thess. iv. 3.

14. Life, ch. 13.

15. Way of Perf. ch. 35.

16. Life, ch. 4.

17. Life, ch. 13.

18. Rib. l. 4, c. 10.

19. "Bonus est Dominus ... animæ quærenti illum."—Lam. iii. 25.

20. Life, ch. 13.

21. "Diligentibus Deum omnia cooperantur in bonum."—Rom. viii. 28.

22. "Etiam peccata."

23. "Omnia possum in eo qui me confortat."—Phil. iv. 13.

24. "Desideria occidunt pigrum."—Prov. xxi. 25.

25. Introd. ch. 37.

26. Found. ch. 28.

27. Way of Perf. ch. 24

28. Life, ch. 39.

29. Spirit, ch. 9.

30. Love of God, B. 12, ch. 8.

31. "Quodcumque facere potest manus tua, instanter operare."—Eccles. ix. 10.

32. "Quia nec opus, nec ratio, nec sapientia nec scientia, erunt apud inferos, quo tu properas."—Ibid.

33. "Et dixi: Nunc cœpi."—Ps. lxxvi. 11.

34. "Perfectum esse non potest nisi singulare."

35. Life, ch. 11.

36. Ibid. ch. 39.

37. "Totum tibi dedit, nihil sibi reliquit."

38. "Pro omnibus mortuus est Christus, ut et qui vivunt, jam non sibi vivant, sed ei qui pro ipsis mortuus est."—2 Cor. v. 15.

39. De Med. cons. 7.

40. Lettre 8.

41. "Seipsum non exhorret, quia nec sentit."—De Cons. l. 1, c. 2.

42. "Consideratio regit affectus, dirigit actus."—Ibid. c. 7.

43. Pall. Hist. laus. c. 98.

44. "In meditatione mea exardescet ignis."—Ps. xxxviii. 4.

45. Life, ch. 8.

46. Ibid. ch. 19.

47. Life, ch. 19.

48. Found, ch. 5.

49. Life, ch. 34.

50. "Hortus conclusus, soror mea sponsa."—Cant. iv. 12.

51. "Venerunt autem mihi omnia bona pariter cum illa."—Wisd. vii. 11.

52. "Non plus sapere, quam oportet sapere, sed sapere ad sobrietatem."—Rom. xii. 3.

53. "Labia enim sacerdotis custodient scientiam, et legem requirent ex ore ejus." —Mal. ii. 7.

54. Lettre 8.

55. "Dilexit nos et tradidit semetipsum pro nobis."—Eph. v. 2.

56. In Cœna D. s. 1.

57. P. 3, q. 79, a. 6.

58. Introd. ch. 20.

59. In 4 Sent. d. 12, q. 3, a. 1, s. 2.

60. Way of Perfection, ch . 35.

61. "Qui semper pecco, semper debeo habere medicum."—De Sacram. l. 4, c. 6.

62. Sitit sitiri Deus."—Tetr. Sent. 37.

63. Sup. Magn. tr. 9, p. 3.

64. Sess. xiii. cap. 8.

65. P. 3. q. 79, a. 1.

66. "Petite, et dabitur vobis; quærite, et invenietis."—Matt. vii. 7.

67. "Oratio cum sit una omnia potest."—Ap. Rodr. p. 1, tr. 5, c. 14; Wisd. vii. 27.

68. "Benedictus Deus, qui non amovit orationem meam et misericordiam suam a me."—Ps. lxv. 20.

69. "Semper obtinemus, etiam dum adhuc oramus."

70. "Dives in omnibus qui invocant ilium."—Rom. x 12.

71. De Dono pers. c. 16.

72. "Necessaria est homini jugis oratio, ad hoc quod cœlum introeat."—P. 3, q. 39, a. 5.

73. " Oportet semper orare, et non deficere."—Luke, xviii. 1.

74. "Sine intermissione orate."—1 Thess. v. 17.

75. Sess. vi. cap. 13.

76. "Hoc Dei donum suppliciter emereri potest."—De Dono pers. c. 6.

77. "Vult Deus rogari, vult cogi, vult quadam importunitate vinci."—In Ps. vi. pœn.

78. "Deus, in adjutorium meum intende; Domine, ad adjuvandum me festina."—Ps. lxix. 2.

79. "Petite, et accipietis."—John, xvi. 24.

80. "Promittendo, debitorem se fecit."—Serm. 110, E. B.

81. "Omnia quæcumque orantes petitis, credite quia accipietis, et evenient vobis."—Mark, xi. 24.

82. "Omnis qui petit, accipit."—Luke, xi. 10.

83. "Oratio in impetrando non innititur merito, sed divinæ misericordiæ."—2. 2, q. 178, a. 2.

84. "Amen, amen, dico vobis: si quid petieritis Patrem in nomine meo, dabit vobi s."—John, xvi. 23.

85. "Si quid petieritis me in nomine meo, hoc faciam."—John, xiv. 14.

86. "Quæramus gratiam, et per Mariam quæramus; quia, quod quærit, invenit, et frustrari non potest."—De Aquæd.

Chapter 5:

1. "Qui plasmasti me, miserere mei."—Vitæ Patr. l. 1.

2. "Si autem impius egerit pœnitentiam, ... omnium iniquitatum ejus, quas operatus est, non recordabor."—Ezech. xviii. 21, 22.

3. "Omnia possum in eo qui me confortat."—Phil. iv. 13.

4. "In te, Domine, speravi; non confundar in æternum."—Ps. xxx. 2.

5. Imit. Chr. B. 3, c. 7.

6. "Discite a me, quia mitis sum et humilis corde."—Matt. xi. 29.

7. Cepar. c. 11.

8. "Tunc exspuerunt in faciem ejus, et colaphis eum ceciderunt; alii autem palmas in faciem ejus dederunt."—Matt. xxvi. 67.

9. "Domine, pati et contemni pro te."

10. Spirit, ch. 10.

11. Imit. Chr. B 3, c. 46.

12. "Mansuetus utilis sibi et aliis."—In Act. hom. 6.

13. Imit. Chr. B. 3, c. 49.

14. Marsol. l. 4, ch. 8.

15. "Beati estis, cum maledixerint vobis, et persecuti vos fuerint, et dixerint omne malum adversum vos mentientes, propter me; gaudete et exultate, quoniam merces vestra copiosa est in cœlis."—Matt. v. 11.

16. "Medicanti irascitur."—In Cant. s. 42.

17. Bacci, l. 2, ch. 17.

18. Way of Perf. ch. 16.

Chapter 6:

1. "Omnis sæculi honor diaboli negotium est."—In Matt. c. 3, n. 5.

2. "Deus superbis resistit; humilibus autem dat gratiam."—James, iv. 6.

3. Way of Perf. ch. 13.

4. "Nec malam conscientiam sanat laudantis præconium, nec bonam vulnerat conviciantis opprobrium."—Contra Petil. l. 3, c. 7.

5. Spirit, ch. 3.

6. Abelly, l. 3, ch. 34, 48.

7. Cepar. c. 13.

8. Way of Perf. ch. 8.

9. "In humiliiate superiores."—Phil. ii. 3.

Chapter 7:

1. "Diliges Dominum Deum tuum ex toto corde tuo."—Matt. xxii. 37.

2. Bacci, l. 22, ch. 15.

3. Avis 36.

4. De Cons. Evang. l. 1, c. 12.

5. "Zelotypus est Jesus."—Ep. ad Eust.

6. "An putatis quoniam inaniter Scriptura dicat: Ad invidiam concupiscit Spiritus qui habitat in vobis?"—James, iv. 5.

7. "Hortus conclusus soror mea, Sponsa."—Cant. iv. 12.

8. Spirit, ch. 9.

9. "Quis dabit mihi pennas sicut columbæ, et volabo, et requiescam?"—Ps. liv. 7.

10. Montée du C. l. 1, ch. 11.

11. "Dilectus metis mihi, et ego illi."—Cant. ii. 16.

12. "Cor mundum crea in me, Deus."—Ps. l. 12.

13. "Qui non renuntiat omnibus quæ possidet, non potest meus esse discipulus." —Luke, xiv. 33.

14. Insin. l. 4, c. 26.

15. "Totum pro toto."—Imit. Chr. B. 3, c. 37.

16. Life, ch. 39.

17. "Bonus est Dominus ... animæ quærenti illum."—Lam. iii. 25.

18. "Regnum mundi et omnem ornatum sæculi contempsi, propter amorem Domini mei Jesu Christi."—Offic. nec Virg. nec Mart. resp. 8.

19. Spirit, ch. 27.

20. "Si dederit homo omnem substantiam domus suæ pro dilectione, quasi nihil despiciet eam."—Cant. viii. 7.

21. Lettres 531, 203.

22. "Introduxit me in cellam vinariam, ordinavit in me charitatem."—Cant. ii. 4.

23. "Ne suscitetis, neque evigilare faciatis dilectam."—Cant. ii. 7.

24. "Summa rerum omnium oblivio."—Reg. fus. disp. int. 6.

25. "Deus meus, et omnia."

26. Imit. Chr. B. 3, c. 34.

27. "Si quis venit ad me, et non odit patrem suum, et matrem, et uxorem, et filios, et sorores, adhuc autem et animam suam, non potest meus esse discipulus."—Luke, xiv. 26.

28. "Et inimici hominis domestici ejus."—Matt. x. 36.

29. 2. 2, q. 104, a. 5.

30. "Frequenter amici carnales adversantur profectui spirituali."—2. 2, q. 189, a. 10.

31. Epist. 111.

32. "Non sine magnis difficultatibus poterit saluti suæ consulere, manebitque in corpore Ecclesiæ velut membrum suis sedibus motum, quod servire potest, sed ægre et cum deformitate. Licet, absolute loquendo, salvari possit, difficile tamen ingredietur viam humilitatis et pœnitentiæ, qua sola ipsi patet ingressus ad vitam."—De Ord. p. 3, c. 1, § 2.

33. "Ab hoc consilio amovendi sunt carnis propinqui ...: in hoc proposito, amici non sunt, sed potius inimici, juxta sententiam Domini: 'Inimici hominis, domestici ejus.'"—Contra retr. a rel. c. 9.

34. "Subdiaconi et diaconi ordinentur ut habentes bonum testimonium et in minoribus Ordinibus jam probati."—Sess. xxiii. cap. 13.

35. "Nullus ordinetur, nisi probatus fuerit."—Cap. Nullus, dist. 24.

36. "Sciant episcopi debere ad hos (sacros) Ordines assumi dignos dumtaxat, el quorum probata vita senectus sit."—Sess. xxiii. cap. 12.

37. "Ut in eis, cum ætate, vitæ meritum et doctrina major accrescat."—Sess. xxiii. cap. 11.

38. "Quia per sacrum Ordinem aliquis deputatur ad dignissima ministeria, quibus ipsi Christo servitur in Sacramento altaris; ad quod requiritur major sanctitas interior quam requirat etiam religionis status."—2. 2, q. 184, a. 8.

39. "Ordines sacri præexigunt sanctitatem; sed status religionis est exercitium quoddam ad sanctitatem assequendam. Unde pondus Ordinum imponendum est parietibus jam per sanctitatem desiccatis; sed pondus religionis desiccat parietes, id est, homines ab humore vitiorum."—2. 2, q. 189, a. 1.

40. "Ut, sicut illi, qui Ordinem suscipiunt, super plebem constituuntur gradu Ordinis, ita et superiores sint merito sanctitatis."

41. "Et ideo præexigitur gratia, quæ sufficiat ad hoc quod digne connumerentur in plebe Christi."

42. "Sed confertur in ipsa susceptione Ordinis amplius gratiæ munus per quod ad majora reddantur idonei."—Suppl. q. 35, a. i.

43. Lib. 6, c. 2, n. 63.

44. "Qui enim se ingerit, et propriam gloriam quærit, gratiæ Dei rapinam facit, et ideo non accipit benedictionem sed maledictionem."—In Hebr. v.

45. "Qui sciens et volens, nulla divinæ vocationis habita ratione, sese in Sacerdotium intruderet, haud dubie seipsum in apertissimum salutis discrimen injiceret."—Sac. Chr. p. 1, c. 4.

46. "Quamvis morum integritas non sit de essentia Sacramenti, est tamen præcepto divino maxime necessaria. ... At vero, quod de idoneitate eorum qui sacris sunt Ordinibus initiandi definitur, non est generalis ilia dispositio quæ in suscipiente quodcumque Sacramentum requiritur, ne sacramentalis gratia obicem inveniat. ... Enim vero, quoniam per sacramentum Ordinis homo, non solum gratiam suscipit, sed ad sublimiorem statum conscendit, requiritur in eo morum honestas et virtutum claritas."—In 4 Sent. d. 25, q. 1, a. 4.

47. "Nesciebatis quæ in his quae Patris mei sunt oportet me esse?"—Luke, ii. 49.

48. "Te autem faciente eleemosynam, nesciat sinistra tua quid facial dextera tua."

—Matt. vi. 3.

49. "Cum oraveris, intra in cubiculum tuum, et clause ostio, ora Patrem tuum in abscondito."—Ibid. 6.

50. "Si quis vult post me venire, abneget semetipsum."—Matt. xvi. 24.

51. "Post concupiscentias tuas non eas, et a voluntate tua avertere."—Ecclus. xviii. 30.

52. "Cesset voluntas propria, et infernus non erit."—In Temp. Pasch. s. 3.

53. "Grande malum propria voluntas, qua fit ut bona tua tibi bona non sint."—In Cant. s. 71.

54. "Unde bella et lites in vobis? nonne hinc, ex concupiscentiis vestris, quæ militant in membris vestris? Concupiscitis, et non habetis."—James, iv. 1, 2.

55. "Unde turbatio, nisi quod propriam sequimur voluntatem?"—De Div. s. 26.

56. Interior Castle, ch. 1.

57. Mont. du C. l. i, ch. 4–13.

Chapter 8:

1. "Discite a me quia mitis sum et humilis corde."—Matt. xi. 29.

2. "Ecce Agnus Dei."—John, i. 29.

3. "Si male locutus sum, testimonium perhibe de malo; si autem bene, quid me cædis?"—John, xviii. 23.

4. "Pater! dimitte illis; non enim sciunt quid faciunt."—Luke, xxiii. 34.

5. "Mansuetorum semper tibi placuit deprecatio."—Judith, ix. 16.

6. "Beati mites, quoniam ipsi possidebunt terram."—Matt. v. 4.

7. "Mansueti autem hæreditabunt terram, et delectabuntur in multitudine pacis ."—Ps. xxxvi. 11.

8. Rib. l. 4, c. 26

9. "Offensiones amoris ipsi escam ministrabunt."

10. "Beati mortui qui in Domino moriuntur."—Apoc. xiv. 13.

11. "Pax Dei, quæ exsuperat omnem sensum."—Phil. iv. 7.

12. "Superabundo gaudio in omni tribulatione nostra."—2 Cor. vii. 4.

13. Lettre 580.

14. "Non in commotione Deus."—3 Kings, xix. 11.

15. Introd. ch. 8.

16. "Unde bella? ... nonne hinc, ex concupiscentiis vestris?"—James, iv. 1, 2.

17. "Ira in sinu stulti requiescit."—Ecclus. vii. 10.

18. "Igne non potest ignis extingui."—In Gen. hom. 58.

19. Lettre 231.

20. "Responsio mollis frangit iram."—Prov. xv. i.

21. "Turbatus præ ira oculus ... rectum non videt."—De Cons. l. 2, c. 11.

22. "Irascimini, et nolite peccare."—Ps. iv. 5.

23. Spirit, ch. 19.

24. Letter 51.

Chapter 9:

1. "Ama, et fac quod vis."

2. "Diliges Dominum Deum tuum ex toto corde tuo."—Matt. xxii. 37.

3. "Domine, quid me vis facere?"—Acts, ix. 6.

4. "Et capillus de capite vestro non peribit."—Luke, xxi. 18.

5. Life, ch. 30.

6. Found, ch. 5.

7. "Ne ventiles te in omnem ventum."—Ecclus. v. 11.

8. Found. ch. 5.

9. "Domine, nonne in nomine tuo prophetavimus, et in nomine tuo dæmonia ejecimus, et in nomine tuo virtutes multas fecimus?"—Matt. vii. 22.

10. "Nunquam novi vos; discedite a me, qui operamini iniquitatem.—Ibid. 23.

11. Entret. 2.

12. "Qui non est paratus omnia pati et ad voluntatem stare dilecti, non est dignus amator appellari."—Imit. Chr. l. 3, c. 5.

13. "Dimitte eum ut maledicat; Dominus enim pnecepit ei ut malediceret David." —2 Kings, xvi. 10.

14. Way of Perfect. ch. 33.

15. "Melior est obedientia, quam stultorum victimæ."—Eccles. iv. 17.

16. Entret. 14.

17. Spirit, ch. 19.

18. Found. ch. 5.

19. Cepar. c. 5.

20. Rev. l. 4, c. 26.

21. Bacci, l. 1, c. 20

22. Bacci, l. 1, c. 20.

23. Introd. p. 1, c. 4.

24. "Quid mihi est in cœlo? et a te quid volui super terram? ... Deus cordis mei, et pars mea, Deus, in æternum."—Ps. lxxii. 25.

25. "Domine quid me vis facere?"—Acts, ix. 6.

Chapter 10:

1. Life, ch. 3.

2. Way of Perf. ch. 12.

3. Vita, c. 14.

4. Part 2, Ep. 54.

5. Love of God B. 9, ch. 2.

6. Life, addit.

7. Ap. Sur. 8 Jul.

8. S. Bas. hom. in Gord. M.

9. "Neque hoc facit stupor, sed amor."—In Cant. s. 61.

10. Life, ch. 25.

11. "Eia, Domine! moriar, ut te videam."—Sol. an. ad D. c. 1.

12. Serm. 85, E. B.

13. "Deus meus, et omnia."

14. "Nihil habentes, et omnia possidentes."—2 Cor. vi. 10.

15. Found. ch. 14.

16. Scala sp. gr. 17.

17. "Beati pauperes spiritu, quoniam ipsorum est regnum cœlorum."—Matt. v. 3.

18. "Habentes autem alimenta et quibus tegamur, his contenti sumus."—1 Tim. vi.

8.

19. De Disc. mon. c. 2.

20. "Avarus terrena esurit ut mendicus, fidelis contemnit ut dominus."—In Cant. s. 21.

21. "Qui volunt divites fieri, incidunt ... in laqueum diaboli et desideria ... nociva, quæ mergunt homines in interitum et perditionem."—1 Tim. vi. 9.

22. Boll. April 26, Act. n. 11.

23. "Non paupertas virtus reputatur, sed paupertatis amor."—Epist. 100.

24. "Pauperes esse volunt, eo tamen pacto, ut nihil eis desit."—In Adv. D. s. 4.

25. Introd. ch. 6.

26. "Dominus pars hæreditatis meæ."—Ps. xv. 5.

27. Cepar. c. 22.

28. "Dominus dedit, Dominus abstulit: sicut Domino placuit, ita factum est; sit nomen Domini benedictum."—Job, i. 21.

29. Life, ch. 22.

30. "Aquæ multæ non potuerunt exstinguere charitatem."—Cant. viii. 7.

31. "Diligentibus Deum omnia cooperantur in bonum."—Rom. vii. 28.

32. "Ab ipso patientia mea."—Ps. lxi. 6.

Chapter 11:

1. "Vanitas vanitatum, et omnia vanitas."—Eccles. i. 2.

2. "Charitas omnia credit."

3. "Beati pauperes.—Beati qui lugent.—Beati qui esuriunt.—Beati qui persecutionem patiuntur.—Beati estis cum maledixerint vobis, ... et dixerint omne

malum adversus vos."—Matt., v. 3–11.

Chapter 12:

1. Summa Theologia I. 2, q. 40, a. 7.]

2. Psalm cxlv. 2

3. Jeremiah xvii. 5

4. Psalm cxviii. 32

5. Isaiah xl. 31

6. 2 Peter i. 4

7. Romans viii. 17

8. Proverbs. viii. 17

9. Lamentations iii. 25

10. Canticle. viii. 5

11. Wisdom. vii. 11

12. Wisdom. vii. 14

13. I. 2, q. 65, a. 5

14. John, xv. 15

15. Love of God, B. 10. c. 10

16. Canticle ii. 16

17. In 3 Sentences d. 26

18. De Trin. l. 8, c. 10

19. Canticles v. 8

20. Genesis xv. 1.

21. De Ver. q. 23, a. 8.

22. Luke, x. 27

23. In 3 Sent. d. 27

24. Matthew xxv. 21

25. Psalm xxxv. 9

26. Ephesians iii. 19

27. Isaiah xxxviii. 17

28. Psalm cxix. 5

29. Psalm xvi. 15

30. Philippians i 23

31. Apophth. 57

32. 2. 2, q. 24. a. 9

33. De Purg. I. 2, c. 7

Chapter 13:

1. James, i. 13

2. 2 Corinthians xii. 7

3. Psalm cxix. 5

4. Psalm cxxiii. 7

5. Tobias xii. 13.

6. In Quadr. s. 5

7. 1 Corinthians. x. 13

8. Matthew vi. 13

9. Conference B. 8, c. 11

10. Psalm lxix. 2

11. De Div. Grat. q. 2, d. 5, § 3.]

12. Matthew xi. 28

13. Psalm xlix. 15

14. Isaiah lviii. 9

15. Ecclesiasticus ii. 12

16. Psalm xvii. 4

17. Isaiah lviii. 9

18. Romans x. 12

19. Wisdom viii 21

20. Epist. ad Eust

21. Vitae Patr. l. 3, n. 35

22. Lib. 6, D. 476

23. Life, addit

24. Mem. de la M. de Chaugy. p. 3. ch. 27

25. Ephesians vi. 11, 12

26. Ephesians vi. 18

27. Psalm xlix. 7

28. Jeremiah xxxiii. 3

29. Luke, xviii. 1

30. Matthew vii. 7

31. Matthew xxvi. 41

32. 1 Thessalonians v. 17

33. In Vig. Nat. s. 3

34. Psalm lxxxviii, 2

35. Introdroduction to Devout Life ch. 13

36. Letter 8

37. Life, ch. 11

38. Spirit, ch. 4

39. Psalm xciii. 19

40. Mem. de la M. de Chaugy, p. 3. ch. 27

41. Love of God, B, 9. ch. 11

Abstract

1. Bacci, 1. 2, ch. 15

2. Imitation of Christ 1. 3. c. 37

www.ingramcontent.com/pod-product-compliance
Lightning Source LLC
Chambersburg PA
CBHW071356120626
46546CB00002B/716